I0119926

Franz Eduard Gehring

# Mozart

Franz Eduard Gehring

**Mozart**

ISBN/EAN: 9783742879080

Manufactured in Europe, USA, Canada, Australia, Japa

Cover: Foto ©Thomas Meinert / pixelio.de

Manufactured and distributed by brebook publishing software
(www.brebook.com)

Franz Eduard Gehring

**Mozart**

# The Great Musicians

*Edited by* FRANCIS HUEFFER

# MOZART

## BY DR. F. GEHRING

### THIRD EDITION

LONDON
SAMPSON LOW, MARSTON & COMPANY
*Limited*
St. Dunstan's House
FETTER LANE, FLEET STREET, E.C.

[*All rights reserved*]

S

KP

*Uniform with this Volume, price 3s. each.*

# THE GREAT MUSICIANS

## A SERIES OF BIOGRAPHIES

EDITED BY

### FRANCIS HUEFFER.

| | |
|---|---|
| **WAGNER.** | **MOZART.** |
| **WEBER.** | **HANDEL.** |
| **SCHUBERT.** | **MENDELSSOHN.** |
| **ROSSINI.** | **SCHUMANN.** |
| **PURCELL.** | **BERLIOZ.** |
| **HAYDN.** | **BEETHOVEN.** |

**CHERUBINI.**

---

**ENGLISH CHURCH COMPOSERS.**

# CONTENTS.

viii CONTENTS.

# MOZART.

WOLFGANG AMADEUS MOZART was the descendant of a family which, towards the close of the sixteenth century, we find settled in Augsburg, where its members earned their livelihood as artists and mechanics. In P. v. Stetten's "History of the Art, Commerce, and Industries of the Imperial Town of Augsburg," mention is made of an Anton Mozart, who painted landscapes with figures in the style of Breughel, selected the costumes of Albrecht Dürer as his models, and was celebrated for the force and durability of his colour. He may be regarded as the founder of the family of Mozart, which, at the beginning of the seventeenth century, had transferred its allegiance from art to the more lucrative pursuit of trade. On the 7th of October, 1708, Johann Georg Mozart, a bookbinder, married Anna Maria Peterin, the widow of Augustin Banneger, whose business Johann Georg had probably carried on for some time. The supporter of the bridegroom and witness of the ceremony was also a Johann Georg Mozart, described as a master mason, and, from the identity of the Christian names, it may be reasonably concluded that he was either the father or uncle of the bridegroom. Three sons were born of this marriage, two of whom, Franz Joseph Ignaz and Franz Alois, followed their father's trade; while the third, Johann Georg Leopold, born November 14th, 1719, became the father of the celebrated Mozart. From his earliest years, Johann Georg Leopold gave proofs of a quick intellect and remarkable strength of purpose in developing his mental capabilities. So imbued was he with the earnest desire of making important progress in his artistic pursuits, that he thought of nothing else, and, in consequence, on his father's death, his brothers, profiting by their mother's feebleness,

B

easily defrauded him of his rights. The Benedictines of
the Convent of St. Ulrich in Augsburg, however, took a
special interest in him. Here he learned music, and soon
became known and esteemed as an organist. A Herr von
Freisinger told Wolfgang Amadeus Mozart in Munich that he
"knew his papa very well, and had heard him when in
Wessobrunn, near Augsburg, play upon the organ with un-
rivalled skill." He added, "It was wonderful to see how his
feet and hands worked away, and certainly unparalleled—
ah! he was indeed a man. My father held him in great
esteem. And how he worried the priests about becoming an
ecclesiastic!" It is evident from this that Leopold Mozart
was destined for the Church by his teachers, the Benedictines,
but he disappointed their intentions. The convent of St.
Ulrich was one of a number of convents founded and partly
maintained by the University of Salzburg. It was probably
on this account that the young man, who was now anxious
to study, went to Salzburg to learn jurisprudence. Here he
had to live with great economy, and, in order to maintain
himself, he was obliged to enter the service of Count
Thurn, a canon of Salzburg Cathedral, as valet.

Whilst in this occupation, he seems to have laid aside his
study of jurisprudence, and to have devoted himself exclusively
to music. He acquired such renown as a violinist, that the
Archbishop Leopold Firmian took him into his orchestra, and
made him court musician. In this orchestra an active part
was taken in the course of time by such distinguished artists
as Eberlin, Michael Haydn, and Adlgasser. Later on Leopold Mozart became court composer and conductor of the
orchestra, and in 1762 the Archbishop Sigismund (Count
Schrattenbach) appointed him vice-capellmeister. The musicians were very badly paid by the archbishop; their
chief inducements to serve him all their lives for little
money seem to have been the provision made for their
widows, the surroundings of the court, and the cheapness
of living at Salzburg. Nearly every day the members of
the orchestra had to play together in church or at court.
Leopold Mozart was one of the most indefatigable. Through
his exertions, according to D. F. Schubart, music was established on an excellent basis. "His style," says Schubart,
"is somewhat antiquated, but profound and rich in contra-

puntal device." His church music was of more value than his chamber music. Indeed, his son declared it to be masterly, even when he had himself become famous for sacred composition. He wished to have some of the pieces performed at Vienna, but his father dissuaded him from the attempt, for he was well aware how tastes had altered in church music. There are still preserved three complete masses, a fragment of a gloria, an offertory, and four litanies, all written for chorus, soli, and orchestra. More numerous by far, however, are his instrumental compositions ; a list published by Marpurg includes thirty serenades alone, besides many symphonies, to one of which his son's name is attached. There are also some occasional pieces, for instance, a pastoral symphony, introducing shepherds' pipes ; military, Turkish, Chinese, and peasant music. In the latter the lyre, the bag-pipe, and the "hackbrett" were to play together. And at in-tervals in the march, a good Salzburg "Juchzer" was to be shouted, and a pistol let off, just as was the custom at the pea-sants' weddings. The "Musikalische Schlittenfahrt" (*Musical sledge-drive*), with a long programme drawn up by Leopold Mozart, and written for the "College of Music " in Augsburg, obtained some celebrity. But it drew forth an anonymous and disparaging letter, which deeply wounded the author. In con-junction with his colleague Eberlin, he composed various pieces for a kind of organ which overlooked the town of Salzburg from the castle hill. These pieces were published in 1759, under the title of " Morning and Evening melodiously and har-moniously announced to the inhabitants of the princely town of Salzburg." Leopold Mozart's activity as a composer was, however, by no means exhausted by the compositions already mentioned. He wrote music for all imaginable instruments. A competent authority says of his pianoforte sonatas, that in listening to them we seem to hear his great son, so strong is the resemblance in form and spirit. Always eager for work in earlier years, he had himself engraved a few of his sonatas in copper. In later times (1778) he tried once more to exercise his old skill, and engraved some " Variations " of his son's.

It is a remarkable coincidence that in the very year when the son afterwards to be so famous was born to him, Leopold Mozart had printed at Augsburg, at his own cost, the work which has carried his own name far and wide : the " Versuch einer gründlichen Violinschule." For a long time this was the only instruction book for the violin which went through numerous editions, and was translated into several languages. To thoroughly appreciate the elder Mozart we must read this book. It displays the greatest thoroughness and variety of ideas, and it abounds in treasures of pedagogic lore. All through he insists on the necessity of the student's becoming thoroughly acquainted with every detail of his art. He must gain an insight into its principles, not trust to chance and accidental taste, but to the laws of nature and art. However highly gifted a man may be by nature, he must study and work hard. Extraordinary natural gifts, no doubt, frequently compensate for the absence of study, but such cases do not affect the universal rule, and by no means lessen the justice of the demands which one makes on every violinist. It was in such principles that he afterwards trained his son.

With the publication of this work Leopold Mozart worthily closed his artistic career. But he continued his onerous duties at church and court just long enough to watch carefully over his children's education, and when his son soon afterwards came out as a composer, he very wisely avoided any rivalry with him. Contemporary critics of the "Violinschule" praise the good German in which it is written. The style is clear; it borders a little on sarcasm and polemics; of hypocrisy, which one might very well have expected from a musician who had so much to do with church dignitaries, there is no trace. Leopold Mozart was indeed a God-fearing man, one who kept God and honour continually before his eyes, but he was free from all bigotry. It is characteristic of him that he was so pleased with the religious poems of Gellert, the Protestant poet, as to write him a letter full of admiration. The poet answered in a long epistle, which has been handed down to us by Nissen, the husband of Wolfgang Mozart's widow, and from which we quote the following passages as being especially worthy of note. "So you read my writings with pleasure, my dear sir, and encourage your friends to read them also? Such a reward, I may tell you candidly, I had scarcely dared to hope for, coming as it does from a source whence I cannot accept it without feelings of vanity. How fortunate I am if I may believe that I have contributed, in some measure, towards the preservation of good taste and good manners even beyond my own country. Has 'Der Christ,' one of my last poems, your approval also? I think I may answer the question myself with 'Yes.' Its subject and your own noble character, which you have unconsciously revealed in your letter, appear to me to warrant this conclusion. I would willingly talk longer with you if I were not on the point of starting for Carlsbad. Commend me to all your friends if they are like you, and how should they be otherwise if they are your friends? You I thank once again for the beautiful, eloquent, and feeling letter with which you have gladdened me." Leopold Mozart certainly had friends, and real friends, as, for instance, the merchant Hagenauer, in whose house he lived some time, and the court trumpeter, Schachtner, from whom we possess the remarkable account of the youthful years of the great Mozart, of which we shall speak more particularly; but such friends form the exception. He must have felt somewhat isolated in Salzburg society from the circumstances of his birth and education. He was unable to associate with the great, although highly esteemed by them as a teacher and musician, and among his equals his strict views of the seriousness of life met with little sympathy. It is observable that the poet who puts the comic figure of Hanswurst (Punch) on the Vienna stage makes him talk in the Salzburg dialect. From time immemorial the Salzburgers have had a taste for low comedy. With them naturally the serious and dignified Leopold Mozart could have nothing in common.

Such was the father of Mozart. He married on the 21st of November, 1747, Maria Anna Pertl, the daughter of Nicolaus Pertl, a subordinate official in Hildenstein, and of Eva Rosina Altmann. Their attachment, according to Leopold Mozart's own confession, was of long standing. "Good things take their time," he adds. An old account informs us that both were so handsome as to be considered in their day the finest couple in Salzburg, and a portrait of Mozart's mother now lying before me quite justifies this admiration as far as she is concerned. An expression of good humour makes it plain to the beholder that Marianne Pertl must have been good tempered, and inclined to take things easily. Indeed a little more energy of character would have been no disadvantage to her. However, Leopold was always at hand if energy were needed. Of seven children which she brought her husband, two only survived, Maria Anne (Nannerl), born July 30th, 1751, and a son born January 27, 1756, at eight o'clock in the evening, who received in baptism on January 28th, at ten o'clock in the morning, the names of Johannes, Chrysostomus, Wolfgangus, Theophilus. The confirmation name of Sigismundus was added later. But Mozart always called himself in after-years Wolfgang Amadé. Johann Theophilus Pergmayr, a tradesman and town-councillor, stood godfather, and the ceremony was performed by the chaplain to the town, Leopold Lamprecht. Wolfgang's birth nearly cost his mother her life, and it was only after a long time that she recovered from the state of prostration which succeeded. As the daughter showed signs of musical talent, her father began to teach her the harpsichord when she was in her seventh year. Wolfgang, too, then scarcely three years old, used to seat himself at the instrument and amuse himself with striking consecutive thirds. He would also try to imitate what he had heard his sister play. When only in his fourth year, his father tried to teach him a few minuets, which he played after him in the most astonishing manner, not merely striking the notes correctly, but also marking the rhythm with firmness and precision. For this information we are indebted to the obituary notice of Schlichtegroll, who had it from the sister Marianne. For each minuet little Wolfgang required half an hour. In his fifth year he attempted the composition of little pieces, which his father wrote down in the same music-book out of which the boy had learnt the minuets. The book is now in the Mozart collection at Salzburg, where it is preserved as the gift of the Princess Helena of Russia. Unfortunately a few pages are missing. At the end of the eighth minuet Mozart's father has written, "The preceding minuets were learnt by Wolfgangerl in his fourth year." Further on we read, "This minuet and trio Wolfgang learned in half an hour on the 26th of January, 1761, the day before his fifth birthday, at half-past nine at night." Against Wolfgang's first composition his father has written, "By Wolfgang Mozart, 11th of May, 1762, and 16th of July, 1762." The sense of perfect form is even here apparent to a remarkable degree. The book accompanied the family in its travels; Wolfgang also wrote down in it his first more important compositions, the sonatas published in the year 1763.

Concerning Mozart's childhood there is no more reliable document than a letter which the court trumpeter, Joh. Andr. Schachtner, wrote soon after Mozart's death to Marianne Mozart, who had married in 1784 the Baron Johann Baptist von Berchthold of Sonnenburg. Schachtner died in 1795, after having filled the post of court trumpeter at Salzburg since 1754. He was a man of considerable literary cultivation, and was even praised by Gottsched for his good German style and his verse. He was very intimate in Mozart's home, and the truth and vividness of the recollections he communicates impress us forcibly in his letter. We read:—" To your first question, ' What was your late brother's favourite amusement in his childhood apart from his occupation of music?' nothing can be answered, for so soon as he began to occupy himself with music, all inclination for other things was as dead in him." This accords with a letter written by Leopold to his son on the 16th of February, 1778, in which he says:—"As a boy you were rather earnest than childlike, and when you sat at the harpsichord, or were otherwise busy with music, no one ventured to jest with you in the smallest degree. Your countenance even was so grave that many intelligent persons, seeing your talent so early developed, and your face always serious and thoughtful, were concerned for the length of your life." "Even childish amusements and games to be interesting to him had to be accompanied by music," writes Schachtner, "and if he and I carried playthings for a game from one room to another, the one who went empty-handed must sing and play on the violin a march all the time." Schachtner's reply to a second question of Marianne's as to how Mozart, when a child, behaved to the great people who admired his talent and skill in music, quite accords with the following passage in Leopold's letter of the 16th of February, 1778 :—" When a boy you were so excessively modest that you cried when you were much praised." To Marianne's third question, " What intellectual occupation did he most prefer?" Schachtner replied, "In this respect he allowed himself to be guided; it was all the same to him whatever they gave him to learn. He was simply willing to learn, but left the choice of subjects to his dearly loved papa." "Next to God comes papa," Mozart used to say when a child. He used to take great delight in the rudiments of mathematics. The somewhat loquacious friend of the family relates a number of anecdotes, all of which tend to show how acutely developed was the boy's sense of sound, and how easily he overcame every technical difficulty. Meanwhile he had also learnt to play the violin. It is related that he could tell when one violin was an eighth of a tone lower than another.

According to Hammerle, an historian of Salzburg, little Mozart made his first appearances in public on the 1st and 3rd of September, 1761, in a Latin comedy "Sigismundus Hungariæ Rex," set to music by Eberlin, the court organist. The school year of the Gymnasium usually closed with these Latin representations. It is interesting to know that little Mozart was chosen for the part of chorister. Nearly a hundred and fifty young people were engaged in the performance as actors and singers. In 1762 Leopold Mozart made his first experiment of a musical tour with both his children. On the 12th of January they travelled to Munich, where they remained three weeks. The children played before the elector, but nothing further is known of this journey. Encouraged by his success, Leopold Mozart asked for leave till Advent, and started on a second tour, the 19th of September, 1762, his destination being Vienna. The whole family travelled first to Passau, where the bishop detained them for five days, as he desired to hear the wonderful child, and then dealt out "a whole ducat," as a mark of gratitude. In company with a canon of the cathedral, Count Herberstein, afterwards Bishop of Passau, they next went to Linz, on the 26th of September. The canon recollected, when many years later he conversed with Leopold Mozart about that time, how Wolfgang had behaved when he saw an old beggar fall into the water. In Linz they gave a concert under the patronage of the governor, Count Schlick. From Linz they went with the so-called "Wasser Ordinaire" passenger-boat down the Danube. When they made a halt at Ybbs, Wolfgang played on the organ in the Franciscan church, and so charmed the fathers that they could not find words of praise enough for him. At the Custom-House at Vienna Wolfgang immediately made up to the official, and played to him on the violin, so much to his delight that the family got through the tedious examination of their luggage in very little time. The court and aristocracy of Vienna had had their curiosity excited with regard to the child prodigy by the Counts Herberstein, Schlick, and Palfy. The imperial family were extraordinarily fond of music. The Empress Maria Theresa, even during the lifetime of her father, Charles VI., himself a talented musician, had studied singing so diligently that she could jokingly say to Faustina Hasse, "she believed herself to be the first of living vocalists." Her daughters were also carefully instructed in singing, and the Emperor Joseph sang well, and played both the harpsichord and violoncello. With a court so favourably disposed towards music, it is not surprising that Leopold, a few days only after his arrival, should have received a command to bring his children on the 13th of October to Schoenbrunn, an imperial palace near Vienna, and this without any solicitation on his part. The children remained three hours with the court, and were then obliged to repeat their performance. The Emperor Francis I., the husband of Maria Theresa, took a peculiar interest in the little " sorcerer."

He made the little fellow play with only one finger, in which he perfectly succeeded. An attempt, which little Mozart made at the special request of the emperor, to play with the keys covered by a piece of cloth, was also a brilliant success. It was, perhaps, owing to the imperial fancy that this species of artistic trick obtained considerable celebrity, and played a not unimportant part in the little sorcerer's répertoire on all his long journeys. Wolfgang entered readily into any joke that was made with him, but sometimes he could be very serious, as, for instance, when he called for the court composer, Georg Christoph Wagenseil, a thorough connoisseur of the harpsichord, and himself a performer. The Emperor stepped back, and made Wagenseil come forward, to whom Mozart said, quite seriously, "I play a concerto by you; you must turn over the pages for me." The Emperor ordered a hundred ducats to be paid to the father. The Empress was very kind to the Mozarts, and sent them costly dresses. "Would you like to know," writes Leopold to Hagenauer, his host at Salzburg, "what Wolferl's (a pet name for Wolfgang) dress is like? It is of the finest cloth, lilac-coloured, the vest of moire of the same colour. Coat and top-coat with a double broad border of gold. It was made for the Hereditary Duke Maximilian Franz." In the picture, which is preserved in the Mozart collection at Salzburg, Mozart is painted in this dress. Wolfgang never showed the least embarrassment in the society of the great. He sprang on to the lap of the Empress Maria Theresa, put his arms round her, and kissed her. The princesses he treated as sisters. He was particularly attached to Marie Antoinette, who once helped him up when he fell on the polished floor, for which he thanked her with the words, "You are good; I will marry you." Nor was he shy with the Crown Prince Joseph; and later, when the latter became Emperor, he reminded Mozart how he had greeted his violin-playing first with "Fie!" then with "That was false!" and at last with "Bravo!" The great world went mad about the children. No musical entertainment could be given without them; they appeared in company with the most celebrated performers. In the midst of this unclouded happiness, Wolfgang was seized with scarlet fever, and for fourteen days was obliged to keep his bed. All passed over happily. Only the great folks held back somewhat for fear of infection. An early return to Salzburg was no longer to be thought of. So on the 11th of December, at the invitation of a Hungarian magnate, the family made an excursion to Pressburg, whence they returned on the 29th of December, in order to be present at a festival which the Countess Kinksy gave in honour of Field-Marshal Daun.

In the first days of the year 1763 the journey back to Salzburg was undertaken, and happily terminated. The Vienna successes encouraged Leopold Mozart to make further plans for similar travels. He had set his mind on reaching Paris and London. In both capitals that great musical movement had already begun which in Germany was developed much later. A great deal has been said about the difficulties which the Archbishop Sigismund threw in the way of the Mozart family. But it deserves to be acknowledged that he gave the father permission for the journey extending over many years, on which the whole family started on the 9th of June, 1763, notwithstanding that in the year previous Leopold had been appointed vice-court-capellmeister.

Paris was to be the next headquarters of the travellers, and on the way thither the father intended to introduce his children at the small German courts. As it was summer our travellers avoided the towns, and generally sought only the country seats, to which the courts removed during the hot season of the year. The journey began with a slight mishap. When in Wasserburg the travelling carriage broke down, enforcing an involuntary day of rest, which, as the father writes to Salzburg, the travellers made good use of by going to the organ, where he instructed his son in the use of the pedal. The child understood it directly, "preferred standing, and used the pedal just as if he had practised it for several months. Every one was lost in astonishment, and this is a new grace of God, which many only receive after much trouble." During this tour Wolfgang was generally no less admired for his organ-playing than for his performances on the harpsichord. On the 12th of June the travellers entered Munich, and went straight to the Residence Nymphenburg, where they were presented to the Elector by the Prince of Zweibrücken. The Elector received them very graciously, and dismissed them with presents. In Augsburg they remained with their relatives a fortnight, and gave three concerts, on the 28th and 30th of June and the 4th of July. "Those who came to the concerts were almost all Lutherans," Leopold writes home. On the 6th of July they left Augsburg, directing their steps through Ulm to Stuttgart. At Plochingen they learnt that the duke was intending to go to his hunting-seat, and they travelled straight by Canstatt to Ludwigsburg in order to meet him there. But in this they were disappointed. Leopold Mozart writes that it was owing to the influence of Jomelli, who was engaged by the duke as capellmeister with brilliant emoluments, that they were obliged to depart without doing anything. "Jomelli is an enemy to all Germans," he observes, "and he has given out that it is scarcely to be credited that a child of German birth should be such a musical genius, and possess so much fire and spirit." Meanwhile it is known of Jomelli that he could appreciate people who were not Italians,—even Germans.

From Ludwigsburg the Mozart family went with introductions from the Prince of Zweibrücken and Duke Clement of Bavaria to the electoral Court at Schwetzingen. "My children have put the whole of Schwetzingen in a ferment. The nobility of the electorate were indescribably pleased, and every one was lost in astonishment." Such was the result of this visit according to Leopold's report. An excursion to Heidelberg was also made. Wolfgang played upon the organ in the Church of the Holy Ghost, and the Dean in remembrance caused his name to be written on the organ. Unfortunately every trace of this monument is lost. At Mayence the children could not play at court on account of the illness of the elector, but they gave three concerts, which brought in two hundred florins. In Frankfort they made such a sensation that they had to supplement the concert given on the 18th of August by three more. On this occasion Goethe, as he in after-years told Eckermann, heard Mozart play :—"I myself was about fourteen, and I can still recollect the little man in his wig and sword quite distinctly." At Coblence they played before the Elector of Treves, and remained some time in the beautiful town, where they found friends in the very musical family of Baron Kerpen. "What will you say when I tell you," writes Leopold Mozart to Hagenauer, "that since we left Salzburg we have already spent one thousand and sixty-eight gulden? But this expenditure has paid in other ways. Besides, for the sake of our health and my genteel reputation we must travel in good style. On the other hand we hold no intercourse with any but noble and distinguished persons, and meet with exceeding politeness and respect." The old man's satisfaction with his success is evident in these words. It was his chief idea to create a kind of position in the world by his children. At Bonn they found the elector absent, and in consequence, after a short stay at Cologne, they continued their journey to Aix-la-Chapelle, where the sister of Frederick the Great, Princess Amalie, received them most graciously. "Only she has no money," writes Leopold. "If the kisses which she gave my children, especially Master

Wolfgang, had been louis-d'ors, we might have been joyful."
At Aix people tried to induce the family to go to Berlin
instead of Paris, but Leopold would not let himself be persuaded out of his resolve, although he was obliged from
Brussels to apply to his friend Hagenauer in Salzburg for a
new letter of credit. After having given a brilliantly successful concert at Brussels under the patronage of Prince
Charles of Lorraine, brother of Mozart's patron, the Emperor
Francis I., they started on their way to Paris, which they
entered on the 18th of November.

Here they found a dwelling in the Hôtel Beauvais, Rue
St. Antoine, the residence of the Bavarian Ambassador,
Count von Eyck, whose wife was a daughter of the High
Chamberlain of Salzburg, Count Arco. The territory of
Salzburg was, at that time, under Bavarian sovereignty,
and on this account also the Mozart family put themselves
under the direct protection of their ambassador. Richly
provided with letters of recommendation they hoped for the
best. "But all the letters came to nothing." Only one
solitary introduction, which the wife of a merchant at Frank-
fort-on-Maine had given Leopold Mozart, brought the family
substantial benefit. It was addressed to the well-known
encyclopædist, Frederick Melchior Grimm, who had lived
in Paris since 1749, as secretary, first to Count Friesen,
and afterwards to the Duke of Orleans, and had access to
the most influential circles. His opinion in musical matters
carried weight. At that time he was neither baron nor
ambassador, but he held it a point of honour to use his political
and literary influence in favour of the Mozarts. Leopold
joyfully writes home:—" He has done everything; he has
introduced the matter at court, and arranged the first
concert (9th of May, 1764). He alone paid me eighty
louis-d'ors, then sold three hundred and twenty tickets, and,
moreover, bore the expense of lighting with wax. We burnt
more than sixty candles. It was he who obtained permission
for the concert, and now he is getting up a second, for which
a hundred tickets have already been distributed. You see
what one man can do who possesses sense and a kind heart.
He is a native of Ratisbon, but has been more than fifteen
years in Paris, and knows how to guide everything in the
right direction, so that all must happen as he intends."

Unfortunately the original account by Leopold Mozart of the family's reception at the Court of Versailles is missing. Marianne Mozart could only recollect in after-years that the Marquise de Pompadour made her brother stand upon a table, that he wanted to kiss her, and when she kept him off, said, " Who is she that she will not let me kiss her ? Yet the Empress kissed me." The king's daughters, especially the Princess Victoire, were very kind to the children, and talked to them, not merely in their own apartments, but also in public.

On New Year's Day, 1764, the Mozart family were conducted to the royal table. Wolfgang stood next the queen, who gave him dainty bits to taste from the table, and talked to him in German, translating the conversation to Louis XV. Near Wolfgang stood his father ; his mother and Marianne were on the other side of the king, where the Dauphin and Madame Adelaide sat. After having played at Versailles, every circle was open to the brother and sister. Gradually Wolfgang's genius became popular. In the " Avantcoureur " of the 5th of March, 1764, we find the following criticism and encomium on Mozart's gifts. It is re-published here for the first time. " M. Mozart, directeur de la musique de S. A. le prince-archevêque de Salzburg est en cette capitale depuis quelques mois avec deux enfans de la plus aimable figure. Sa fille, âgée de onze ans, joue du clavessin d'une manière distinguée, on ne sçaurait avoir une exécution plus exacte et plus brillante. Son fils, qui a en ce mois-ci sept ans accomplis, est un vrai prodige. Il a tous les talens et toute la science d'un maître de chapelle. Non seulement il exécute d'une manière surprenante les concerts dès maîtres les plus célèbres de l'Europe, mais il compose lui-même. Il joue de tête pendant des heures entières, et se livrant à l'inspiration de son génie, il associe les idées les plus précieuses à la science de l'harmonie la plus profonde. Tous ceux qui sçavent ce que c'est la musique sont restés dans la dernière surprise à voir faire à un enfant ce qu'ils auraient admiré dans le maître de chapelle le plus consommé. On peut mettre cet enfant étonnant à toutes les épreuves. Qu'on lui donne un morceau sans basse, et qu'on exige qu'il écrive la basse dessous, il le fera sans avoir besoin de clavessin ni de violon, dont peu de compositeurs se peuvent passer en écrivant. Qu'on lui donne une partie de violon, il la jouera sur le clavessin et y mettra tout de suite la basse qu'il lui faudra. Souvent il fera même entendre les parties intermédiaires. Il accompagnera d'oreille des airs qu'on chantera devant lui, et il les variera même sur le champ d'une infinité de manières. Il a une si grande habitude du clavier qu'on peut étendre une serviette dessus sans que cela l'empêche de jouer avec la même exactitude et la même vitesse. Ces enfans ont eu l'honneur de jouer plusieurs jours de suite devant monseigneur le Dauphin, madame la Dauphine, et mesdames de France, ainsi que devant un grand nombre de personnes de distinction de la cour et de la ville. Le jeune Mozart a aussi eu l'honneur de jouer des orgues dans la chapelle du Roi à Versailles pendant une heure et demie en présence de cette auguste assemblée."

On the 10th of March, soon after the appearance of this article, which gives us an exact idea of Wolfgang's skill, the family, with Grimm's assistance, gave a concert in the theatre of M. Felix, Rue St. Honoré, at which they took a hundred and twelve louis-d'ors. A second concert on the 9th of April, a kind of farewell performance, brought in still more. "The permission to give both these concerts," writes Leopold, " is something quite unusual, and in direct opposition to the privileges granted to the Opera, to the ' Concert spirituel,' and to the French and Italian theatres." The permission was only obtained from M. de Sartines, Lieutenant-general of Police, by embassies and private letters from the Duc de Chartres, the Duc de Durat, Count Tessé, and many great ladies. Marianne, too, met with warm approbation at these concerts. She played the compositions of two masters then popular in Paris, Schobert of Strasburg, and Eckart of Augsburg, with as much clearness and precision as those masters themselves. Both brother and sister were naturally loaded with presents and commendations. A talented amateur, Count de Carmontelle, painted the gifted family. Wolfgang is seated in a portico playing on the harpsichord; his father stands behind him leaning against his chair, and accompanying him on the violin; his sister stands on the other side of the harpsichord, turning towards him, and singing from a music-book. The picture has been made generally known by a well-preserved engraving of De la Fosse. There is another picture of Mozart which represents him in the midst of a brilliant company. It is a small oil-painting which formerly belonged to the Duc de Rohan-Chabot, and now hangs in the gallery of Versailles. During the sojourn of the family in Paris, Wolfgang's first compositions were published by his father. They were two sonatas (Nos. 6 and 7 in Köchel's catalogue) dedicated to the Princess Victoire; and two others (8 and 9 in Köchel) dedicated to the Countess de Tesse, maid of honour to the Dauphiness. We can perfectly agree even nowadays with the father's opinion that these sonatas were good, and not merely so because a child had composed them. They are remarkable for their novelty of ideas and ingenuity of form.

If France had hitherto rendered considerably more homage and enthusiasm to Wolfgang's youthful and aspiring genius than his fatherland, it was reserved to England, whither the family now turned their steps, to enter still more deeply into the true spirit of this young master. Leopold was right when he observed in letters written from England, "It passes all imagination. What he knew when we left Salzburg is a mere shadow compared with what he now knows." Wolfgang had indeed learnt much, even during his Paris sojourn, and certain circumstances in England contributed still more to develop his talent.

On the 10th of April, the day following the second concert at the theatre of M. Felix, the family left Paris. They made a stay at Calais, where they were invited to dine with the Procureur du Roi et de l'Amirauté, and where they left their travelling-carriage. They greatly enjoyed watching the tides: —"How the sea runs away and grows again!" writes Marianne in her journal. As the packet-boat was overcrowded, Leopold hired a private vessel for five louis-d'ors, on which, besides his own family and servants, he was able to take four other passengers, who each contributed half a louis. Two servants accompanied the family, one of whom, an Italian, named Porta, acted as courier, and made the best arrangements he could for them on their travels. The passage was good. "We are happily across the brook of Maxglan" (a little river near Salzburg). Old Leopold suffered most from sea-sickness. On nearing the cliffs of Dover, they found it necessary to go on board a smaller vessel in order to land conveniently, and for this accommodation they had to pay a further sum of six laubthalers—about thirty shillings.

On the 23rd of April, the Mozarts arrived in London, and took lodgings in the house of a hair-dresser named Couzins, in Cecil Court, St. Martin's Lane. The dress of the people, made a peculiar impression on the family. However, they hastened to adopt English customs. "How do you suppose," writes Leopold to Hagenauer, "my wife and girl look in English hats, and the great Wolfgang in English clothes?" As early as the 27th of April, they had the honour of being permitted to play before the king and queen at Buckingham House, from six to nine in the evening. "The kindness shown to us by both those exalted personages is beyond description," writes the father. "We could not have supposed from their friendly manner that they were the king and queen of England. We have met with extraordinary politeness at every court, but what we have experienced here surpasses all the rest." Eight days afterwards, as the family were walking in St. James's Park, the king and queen came to drive there, and, although the Mozarts were all differently dressed, recognized them when they made their bow. The king opened the carriage window, put his head out, and smilingly returned the salutation, bowing and waving his hands especially to "our master Wolfgang." George III., like his consort, the Princess Charlotte Sophia of Mecklenburg-Strelitz, was very fond of music, and particularly of Handel's. He maintained his orchestra, the "King's Band," and the choir of the Chapel Royal. But Wolfgang was now to play for the first time in public. On the 9th of May, it was announced in the "Public Advertiser" that the violoncellist Graziani would give a concert on the 17th at Hickford's Rooms in Brewer Street, and that at this concert would be performed "concerts on the harpsichord by Master Mozart, who is a real prodigy of nature; he is but seven years of age, plays anything at first sight, and composes amazingly well. He has had the honour of exhibiting before their majesties greatly to their satisfaction." The concert, however, had to be postponed to the 22nd. In the meantime, after playing with his sister for the second time at court on the evening of the 19th, young Mozart became unwell, and Graziani's concert took place without his assistance. For each performance at court the family received the sum of twenty-four guineas. At the second performance, the king was more delighted than ever with the "prodigy of nature;" he had placed before him pieces by Wagenseil, Bach, Abel, and Handel. "He played them all at sight," writes the father. "His performance on the king's organ was such that every one rates his organ-playing far higher than his playing on the harpsichord. Afterwards he accompanied the queen in an aria which she sang, and played on the *flauto traverso* in a solo. Lastly he took up the violin parts of Handel's arias which accidentally lay there, and over the plain bass played the most beautiful melodies, so that every one was lost in the utmost amazement." Here follows the enthusiastic comparison quoted above of the progress which Wolfgang had made in the last year since he quitted Salzburg.

In announcing the first concert of the two children, Leopold Mozart says, "His father brought the boy to England nothing doubting of his success in a land where his countryman Handel enjoyed such peculiar protection during his life." The concert was fixed for the 5th of June, the day after the king's birthday. Many families of position which had already left town had returned for the royal birthday. The public holiday was celebrated with a grand illumination, and on the following day the Earl of Northumberland arranged a private fete, at which fifteen hundred guests were present, and ten thousand lamps lighted in the gardens of the palace. It was on this day that the first concert took place. The receipts amounted to nearly a hundred guineas, and the expenses gave Leopold no cause for uneasiness, for most of the musicians who assisted would accept no pay. "If I had not actually seen and heard it, I could not have believed it," exclaims the delighted father, "even all you in Salzburg can form no idea of it, for it is quite another thing now." On the 29th of June, Wolfgang performed in the saloon at Ranelagh for the benefit of a public charity, apparently the Lying-in Hospital on the Surrey side of Westminster Bridge. After this concert the family intended travelling to Tunbridge, but they must have been back again before the end of July, for on the 3rd of August Leopold writes of an illness from which he is suffering, the result of a cold caught in riding home from a concert given at the house of the Earl of Thanet. On the 6th of August, he removed with his children to Chelsea, where he took up his abode in the house of Dr. Randal in Five Fields Row, now Lower Ebury Street. Here he remained seven weeks. Out of consideration for his state of health no instrument could be touched, so Wolfgang was obliged to make up for this deprivation by composing. He began to write symphonies for orchestra. His sister, who used to sit by him, relates of that time that he said to her, "Remind me that I give the French horn plenty to do." This instrument was then a favourite in England, and for some time we find it a prominent feature in Wolfgang's early works. It was thus that his first symphonies originated, and even at that early date we find them marked by an artistic sense of form and connexion. The chief advantage of these attempts, however, was that Wolfgang remained in practice, and was able to announce that at the next concert all the instrumental works would be of his composition. While in Chelsea Leopold Mozart made the acquaintance of the violoncellist Siprutini. He was the son of a Dutch Jew, and his new friend sought to awaken in him an artist's interest in the Catholic Church. He succeeded in making him acknowledge that of all the Christian forms of belief the Catholic was the best, and he hoped to accomplish still more. But he got no further. When Leopold was sufficiently recovered to remove to town, the family went to lodge at Mr. Williamson's in Thrift Street, now Frith Street, Soho. Once again they were invited to court on the 25th of October, the anniversary of the king's accession to the throne. But the favourable time for a pecuniary success was over, especially as Leopold Mozart found himself in a measure obliged to have six sonatas of Wolfgang's, for harpsichord and violin, printed, in order to dedicate them to the Queen. These sonatas and others of his early works have long been contemptuously overlooked, yet they are, in their way, works of art even in a higher degree than the works of many maturer artists.

About this time Wolfgang received his first thorough instruction in singing. His teacher was Giovanni Manzuoli, a celebrated soprano, who made his appearance in London at the Italian opera, which opened on the 24th of November, 1764. Wolfgang also derived much advantage from listening to Tenducci the celebrated soprano. When next year he again visited Grimm in Paris, the latter heard Wolfgang sing, and observed that he had profited so well by studying with Manzuoli, that, although his voice was feebler, yet he sang with as much taste and feeling as Manzuoli himself. So we see that to Mozart knowledge came easily, and that he was early familiar with that experience which other composers only acquire late in life or perhaps never.

In 1765, on the 21st of February, the brother and sister appeared again at a concert which ought to have taken place on the 15th, but had been postponed on account of Dr. Arne's oratorio "Judith." The receipts were satisfactory enough. After repeated announcements, the concert at last took place on the 13th of May, and Wolfgang played on a harpsichord with two manuals, built for the King of Prussia by Burkhard Tschudi. From this time Leopold Mozart invited the public, by frequent advertisements in the papers, to come and hear the children in private every day from twelve to three o'clock, admission from half-a-crown. These private performances were given first at their own rooms, and afterwards at the Swan and Hoop Tavern in Cornhill. However, the visitors became scarcer and scarcer. The last announcement of this kind appeared in the "Public Advertiser" of the 11th of July. The talents and performances of the boy prodigy were put to repeated proofs by Danes Barrington, a fellow of the Royal Society, who afterwards published a detailed account of them in "Philosophical Transactions of the Royal Society." With great conscientiousness he had first obtained Wolfgang's certificate of baptism. After the usual experiments in playing at sight, he requested the boy to improvise a love-song nearly as Manzuoli would sing it. Wolfgang instantly began an introductory recitative, which was followed by an air on the word "affetto." The pendant was formed by a passionate song on the word "perfido." Barrington reported that these compositions were far above the average. From this we may infer that the boy observed the rules of composition with a certain freedom. It is interesting, moreover, to note that even at that time he knew how to give a definite form to certain dramatic motives. In this respect the air for tenor (21, Köchel), composed in London in 1765, is remarkable. During the last weeks of their stay in London the family made frequent visits to the British Museum, to which Wolfgang presented his printed sonatas and an autograph copy of a short madrigal for four voices, "God is our Refuge," apparently on a given melody. The secretary, Mr. Maty, addressed a letter of thanks for these gifts to little Mozart on the 19th of July, 1765.

On the 24th of the same month, the family left London. They spent one day in Canterbury, and the remainder of the month with Horatio Man at his estate of Bourne. On the 1st of August they left England, travelling by way of Calais to the Hague, whither they were proceeding on the invitation of the Princess Caroline of Nassau-Weilburg. But their journey met with an interruption at Lille, for Wolfgang became dangerously ill, and they were obliged to make a stay there of four weeks. At the end of this time they continued their journey through Ghent, and first entered the Hague in September. Here it was Marianne's turn to be ill, so ill indeed that the last sacrament was administered to her. "Had any one heard the conversations which I and my wife and daughter had, and how we convinced the latter of the vanity of the world, and of the blessed death of children, he would certainly not have been without moist eyes, while Wolfgang in another room was occupied with his music." But the skilful treatment of Professor Schwenkel, physician-in-ordinary to the Princess of Weilburg, saved Marianne.

The new year, 1766, had a fresh calamity in store for them —Wolfgang fell sick of a violent fever. To satisfy in some measure the boy's intellectual cravings, they had to place a board across his bed, on which he could write. An air for soprano (" Conservati fedele," 23, Köchel) was the result of these days (written at the Hague in January, 1766). This air contains curious turns of harmony. A symphony in B major was also finished here, in which are observable the elements of a thematic development. At Amsterdam, where the family remained four weeks, they were, notwithstanding its being Lent, permitted to give concerts, " because the publishing abroad of the marvellous gift of this child serves to the glory of God:" so runs the decree of the Calvinistic magistrate. They were soon called back to the Hague for the ceremonies in connexion with the coming of age of the Prince of Orange, on the 8th of March, 1766. Wolfgang was commissioned to compose six sonatas (26—31, Köchel) for the princess, which were straightway printed with a dedication. He had also to write other trifles, amongst them variations for the harpsichord upon the hymn composed for the installation festival (24, Köchel), and upon another melody "which is sung, played, and whistled by everybody in Holland." This is the song composed by Philipp von Marnix for the Prince of Orange, Wilhelmus van Nassau, the proper Dutch national hymn. For a concert opportunely given during the festivities, Wolfgang composed an orchestral piece, a sort of overgrown concerto, even the harpsichord obbligato appeared in it; he called it "Galimathias musicum." Sketches for it in Wolfgang's hand, corrected by his father, are still in existence. The horns take a prominent part in this work. It is also remarkable for an imitation of the bagpipes. The last of the thirteen very short and mostly bipartite movements is rather more extended, being partly a fugue, partly a free imitation, with the first part of the national air "Wilhelmus van Nassau" for a subject. A publisher of Haarlem brought out for the installation festival of the Prince of Orange a Dutch translation of Leopold Mozart's "Violinschule," which he dedicated to the prince. On the occasion of the presentation of this translation to Leopold, which took place the day after the festival, Wolfgang was invited to play on the famous Haarlem organ. Soon afterwards the family travelled through Mechlin, where they visited their friend the Archbishop Johann Heinrich, Count of Frankenberg, to Paris. It is observable that Leopold Mozart chose by no means the shortest route, for he was continually on the look-out for increasing as much as possible his son's youthful reputation.

On the 10th of May the Mozarts entered Paris once more, and went to live in lodgings procured for them by Grimm. In Grimm's opinion both daughter and son had made important progress, and this view was generally shared. Meanwhile, however, the public appears to have taken a less lively interest in the wonderful children than on the occasion of their first visit to Paris. They played several times at Versailles. The daughter of the Duke of Orleans, whom Joseph II. wished to marry, and who afterwards espoused the Prince de Condé, "took the liberty" of dedicating a little rondo for harpsichord and violin of her own composition to Wolfgang. The hereditary Prince Karl Wilhelm Ferdinand von Braunschweig, who had won great laurels in the Seven Years' War, sought out the family. "He is a very pleasant, handsome, friendly gentleman, and, on entering, questioned me instantly whether I were the author of the 'Violinschule,'" writes Leopold Mozart. Grimm relates that the hereditary prince, speaking of Wolfgang, said that many a finished capellmeister in the profession might die without having learnt what this boy of nine years old knew. Wolfgang had again to enter into competition with the most distinguished performers on the harpsichord and the organ. He always acquitted himself honourably on these occasions, and sometimes triumphantly. There is an interesting composition of the time of this Paris visit—a Kyrie, the earliest of Wolfgang's sacred works—which has been preserved. The vocal parts proceed equally throughout; still the piece is interesting on account of its beautiful sound, and a few rare modulations. It gives us a glimpse, too, of the great talent of the composer in this particular direction.

On the 16th of August Leopold writes home from Lyons that the family had left Paris on the 9th of July, and had then proceeded to Dijon, where the Duc de Condé had invited them in order that they might appear before the persons of quality there assembled. At Dijon they remained fourteen days. At Lyons they made a longer stay, lasting four weeks, principally on account of a merchant and amateur Meurikofer. Wolfgang took the greatest delight in hearing this gentleman sing an Italian song, with spectacles on his nose. The journey was then continued by way of Geneva to Lausanne. It is not likely that the Mozarts sought admittance to Voltaire in Ferney, as is presumed by Edmond von der Straeten, and by the author of the article on Mozart in Grove's Dictionary. But it is very possible that Voltaire's friends in Lausanne, where the Mozarts spent five days, made inquiries at Ferney as to whether such a visit would be welcome. Among Leopold's patrons in Lausanne, besides Prince Ludwig von Würtemberg, were Madame d'Autbonne, Madame d'Hermenche, and M. de Severy. "The prince was still with us," writes Leopold, "when we were already in the carriage, and I had to promise him, with a shake of the hand, that I would write to him often and give him news of our circumstances."

In Berne a stay of eight, and in Zurich of fourteen days was made. As early as the beginning of October, the family left Zurich, and for the first time, in November, Voltaire mentions in a letter "a young player on the harpsichord whom he had not been able to hear on account of illness." Can this have been Mozart, the same Mozart who afterwards in such a remarkably unsympathetic manner expressed himself on the subject of Voltaire's death? The Mozarts must have passed by Ferney in the first days of September, and Voltaire first refers to the subject in November! At Zurich the Mozarts formed an intimacy with Salomon Gesner, who gave them his works, with a particularly cordial inscription as a remembrance. From Zurich they travelled by way of Winterthur and Schafhausen, where they remained four days, to Donaueschingen. Here they were expected by Prince Josef Wenceslaus of Fürstenberg. The director of music, Councillor Martelli, came immediately with compliments and invitations. For twelve days there were musical performances every evening from five till nine o'clock. "We perform something special each time," writes Leopold. The family *répertoire*, at this rate, must have been tolerably extensive. "If the year were not so far advanced," he continues, "they would not let us go. The prince gave me twenty-four louis-d'or, and each of my children a diamond ring. The tears ran down his cheeks when we took leave; we, too, all wept. He begged me to write to him often." The next stage of the journey was through Mösskirch to Biberach. Here Count Fugger von Babenhausen made Wolfgang enter the lists of organ-playing with Sixtus Bachmann, a boy only two years older than himself. "Each did his utmost to dispute the other's superiority, and both came honourably out of the competition," such is the report of a contemporary.

Travelling through Ulm, Günzburg, and Dillingen, the Mozarts entered Munich on the 8th of November. Next day the elector desired the children to appear before him, and was much pleased when Wolfgang composed, during dinner, a little piece for which he had himself given the motive. At this time Wolfgang was once more attacked by illness, and an intended visit to Prince Thurn and Taxis at Regens-burg had to be given up. The last letter written by Leopold to Salzburg during this journey is dated the 22nd of November. He writes : " It is very important that there should be a home-life for me specially devoted to my children. God (who is only too good to me, miserable wretch that I am) has given my children such talents as, setting aside my obligations as a father, would incite me to sacrifice every-thing to their good education. Every moment that I lose is lost for ever, and if I ever knew how valuable time is in youth I know it now. You know that my children are used to work. If they were to get into idle habits on the pretext that one thing or another, for ins*ance, in the home and its concerns, hindered them, my whole structure would fall to the ground. Habit is an iron path, and you know yourself how much my Wolfgang has still to learn. But who knows what is in store for us at Salzburg? Perhaps we shall be received in such a manner that we shall most gladly throw our bundles over our shoulders again. At any rate I am bringing my children back to their fatherland, God willing. If they are not welcome, it is not my fault. But they cannot be had for nothing." This letter indicates the position of Leopold Mozart and his two children on their return from the tour which had lasted three years and a half, in the most striking manner. The archbishop's capellmeister might well feel somewhat uneasy at the thought of returning home after having more than once exceeded his leave of absence. The man who had been naturalized, as it were, in the society of the great ones of this earth, might well possess a certain pride in the accomplish-ments of his children as in his own work, and we can under-stand the effort it would cost him to accommodate himself once again to the simple circumstances of his life at Salzburg. But, on the other hand, we cannot help admiring the sound, common sense which saw so plainly into the future, and which recognized that the children's education had yet to be begun, and to what an extent it must be carried in order to bring their remarkable talents to full development and maturity.

At the end of November the family came home. Besides numerous presents and not inconsiderable gains, the parents had the great good-fortune to bring the children back in excellent health and spirits, notwithstanding the severe illnesses they had had. It is no less satisfactory to know that Wolfgang had preserved a childlike mind. As Marianne in after-years related, he rode merrily about the room on his father's stick, and played just as in the old days with his favourite cat, which Frau Hagenauer had taken care of during the absence of the family. While travelling about he had created for himself an imaginary kingdom, which he called "Rücken." It was to be inhabited by children, of whom he was to be the king. His idea of this kingdom was so distinct, that a servant had to draw him a map of the places to which he gave the names. During the absence of the Mozarts, their landlord's son, Dominicus Hagenauer, had turned monk. When Wolfgang heard of it, he was so grieved that he cried bitterly, because he thought he should never see him again. He was quieted at last, and formed the design of going immediately upon his return home to the monastery of St. Peter, to let Dominicus catch him some flies and shoot with the cross-bow. His droll fancies were many, and his presence of mind in giving appropriate answers was astonishing. A great man (perhaps the archbishop himself) once said to him, "We have been to France and England, we have been presented at court, we have gained honour." Suddenly Wolfang interrupted him with, "But I don't remember, sir, having seen you anywhere but here in Salzburg."

As soon as they were a little settled, Leopold began to instruct his son thoroughly in counterpoint, taking Fux's "Gradus ad Parnassum" as the groundwork of his teaching. He possessed a copy of the original Latin edition of this celebrated work, and as the boy doubtless became acquainted with this copy, he must also have learned in this way the rudiments of Latin. In the Mozarteum at Salzburg there is preserved a copy-book with exercises in thorough bass and counterpoint, in which the old chorales chosen as *canto fermo* are borrowed from the "Gradus ad Parnassum." Soon Wolfgang had an opportunity of making practical use of his knowledge. As Barrington relates, in his article which appeared in "Philosophical Transactions," and which has been already referred to in these pages, the Archbishop of Salzburg was somewhat incredulous concerning the boy's marvellous gifts, and, in order to test them, had him shut up alone for a week, with orders to compose an oratorio, the text for which he gave him. Wolfgang passed the ordeal brilliantly. This was towards the end of 1766. The text of the oratorio, which was destined for Lent 1767, was printed at Salzburg by Johann Josef Mayrs, "Court and University printer and publisher, 1767," and is entitled, "The obligation of the first and chief commandment. Mark xii. 30. 'Thou shalt love the Lord thy God with all thy heart, and with all thy soul, and with all thy mind, and with all thy strength,' expounded by J. A. W. First part set to music by Herr Wolfgang Motzard (sic) aged ten. Second part by Herr Joh. Mich. Heiden (sic) the eminent concertmeister. Third part by Herr Anton Cajetan Adlgasser, the eminent composer of chamber-music and organist. Scene : A beautiful country, with a garden and little wood. Voices : A secret, but afterwards zealous, Christian ; the Spirit of Christ, the Spirit of the World, Divine Charity, Divine Justice." The introduction begins in the following manner :—" Divine truth assures us in the mysterious revelation of John, that there is no more dangerous condition of the soul than that of luke-warmness in the concerns of salvation, &c. This is taken as the motive of the musical representation, a representation which seeks not merely to charm the senses, but also usefully to entertain the mind."

Mozart's original manuscript bears the title in his father's handwriting : "Oratorium di Wolfgango Mozart composto nel mese di Marzo 1766." "March" is an error, for at that time the family were still travelling in the Netherlands. It must refer to the date of the performance, which took place in the *Aula* of the University of Salzburg on the 12th of March, 1767, at half-past six in the evening. This circumstance makes it probable that the oratorio, which was intended for the Lent of 1767, was composed in the last weeks of 1766, soon after the return of the Mozarts to Salzburg. A repetition of the performance took place on the 2nd of April, 1767. We should, perhaps, have known nothing further of the work than the title, if the Prince Consort had not bought the original score of this, the first dramatic attempt of Mozart, from André's collection, and deposited it in the Royal Library, Windsor. The manuscript was copied by C. F. Pohl at Windsor, and the work

is now included in the complete edition of Mozart's works
published by Breitkopf and Härtel. One of the first-fruits of
Mozart's genius, it is noticeable for his efforts to make it
characteristic ; the chromatic scale plays a very considerable
part in it, and we cannot but admire the way in which the
boy has illustrated by the music the resurrection at the day
of judgment. The *recitativo secco* no longer satisfies him ;
his obbligato recitative already assumes larger proportions.
Among the seven arias which occur in it, there is one for
tenor, which may be regarded as a work of art, so finished is
the melody, so refined and expressive the instrumentation.
It would seem, too, that Mozart himself placed a high value
on this aria, for in the following year he introduced it into
his first opera—the only instance known in which Mozart has
borrowed from himself, although the habit of borrowing
was very common among other composers. There is a little
"Passion" cantata for two voices (Köchel, 42), also written
for the Lent of 1767, which shows us that "young
Orpheus" was quite familiar with the chord of the minor
seventh.

How much Mozart was liked wherever he went, his intercourse with the monks of the monastery of Seeon tends to
prove. Soon after his return from Paris he made an excursion there. The monastery can be reached in an hour from
the northern shore of the Chiem lake ; it lies on the shores of
a small lake, and is now the property of the Empress of Brazil.
One day at table the prelate observed that an offertory was
wanted for the Feast of Benediction, the 21st of March. A
little while after Wolfgang left the refectory, and in a few
minutes wrote down on a window-sill the offertory, "Scande
cœli limina," the calm, soft, gliding melody of which is
continued through a long passage for the violin. Wolfgang
was very friendly with Father Johannes (a Herr von Haasy).
He had a special melody for the words, "Mein Hanserl (a
diminutive of Johannes) lieb's Hanserl erfordern," with which
he always greeted the father when he met him.

Wolfgang's talent was in request for another public festival
in Salzburg, during the year 1767. As has been already
mentioned, when referring to the "first appearance of Mozart,"
it was customary for the school year to close with a Latin
play acted by the students. The tragedy, "Clementia Croesi,"

was fixed upon for the 13th of May, 1767. It was to be preceded by a musical prologue, "Apollo and Hyacinthus," or "The Transformation of Hyacinth," the composition of which was undertaken by the "nobilis dominus, Wolfgangus Mozart, undecennis." We gather from this work that Wolfgang was still struggling with his Latin. It displays far less originality than the oratorio, still it is curious to observe in it the facility with which Wolfgang mastered the conventional form of Italian opera, on which this Latin school comedy was modelled.[1]

In the summer of 1767 the Mozarts started on a new tour. Wolfgang composed for this tour four pianoforte concerti, which are interesting on account of the efforts observable in them to blend into an harmonious whole the orchestra and the solo part. The motive which prompted the new tour, having Vienna for its destination, was the approaching marriage of the Archduchess Maria Josepha with King Ferdinand of Naples. This occasion Leopold hoped might prove an opportunity for adding to his children's fame, and for bringing them into notice at the court. On the 11th of September they set out, Frau Mozart also accompanying them, and made only short stays at Lambach and Melk. At Vienna misfortune befell them, for the Princess-bride was seized with small-pox in the beginning of October, and died on the 15th, the "name-day" of the Empress. The small-pox became an epidemic, and Leopold Mozart fled with his children to Ollmuetz. But in vain, for both Wolfgang and Marianne were attacked by the fearful disease. Fortunately for them the kindly-disposed and brave Dean of Ollmuetz, Count Leopold Anton von Podstatzky (also a canon of Salzburg), received the family into the deanery, where the children were carefully tended. The disease took a very violent form. Wolfgang lay for nine days blind. Every day the archbishop's chaplain, Hay, visited the family, and, when they began to recover, amused the children with card-tricks, which Wolfgang learned from him. As convalescence advanced Wolfgang learned to fence. On the journey back to Vienna, the Mozarts stayed a fortnight with Count Schrattenbach, brother of the Archbishop

[1] At the representation Wolfgang himself accompanied on the harpsichord.

of Salzburg, and were treated with much distinction by the nobility of Brünn.

At the beginning of January, 1768, the family reached Vienna once more. But here they found things greatly altered. Maria Theresa, it is true, received them very graciously, and made Frau Mozart tell her all about the children's illness, entering into every detail; the Emperor Francis I., too, was most courteous, but he had established a system of such economy that no commands were issued for the Mozarts to play at court. Whilst in former times no aristocratic gathering took place at which artists and performers were not in the greatest request, now the only pleasure seemed to be in balls which were arranged on a system of mutual contribution. At that time, in Vienna no one seemed to care particularly for music. In Wolfgang, the child prodigy, the public had indeed shown some interest; to Wolfgang, the budding artist, they were, alas, indifferent. Leopold Mozart complained bitterly of this state of things in his letters to Salzburg. Moreover the jealousy displayed by other musicians towards the Mozarts was well-nigh intolerable. Life became a burden to them. Intrigues and envious calumnies were abundant. Meanwhile the Emperor sided with the Mozarts, and proposed that Wolfgang should write an opera; he desired, too, that the youthful composer should himself direct his work at the harpsichord. Naturally father and son assented willingly to this proposition. "But what quarrels broke out among the composers!" writes Leopold. "What! shall we see to-day a Gluck, and to-morrow a boy of twelve seated at the harpsichord and direct his opera himself? Yes, in spite of all jealousies! I have even brought Gluck himself over to our side, so far that, if he does not enter into it quite heartily, he will not let it be perceived, *for our protectors are also his.*" Unfortunately the Emperor had no final voice in the concerns of the opera, for it was leased to the *impresario* Affligio. Still the imperial wish went for something, especially as Affligio's singers supported it. Leopold Mozart, therefore, concluded an agreement for his son with Affligio, by which the former was to compose an opera for a hundred ducats. Serious opera was not much affected by the society of Vienna. At the representation of Gluck's "Alceste," angry words were to be heard among the audience: "This is edifying! Nine days without a play, and on the tenth a 'De Profundis.' What! I fancy this is intended for tears. Possibly I may shed some through being bored. No! it is throwing money away! a delightful spectacle! a fool who dies for her husband!" Then, too, the singers of serious opera were not satisfactory, while on the other hand those of opera-buffa were superior. So that Wolfgang was to have an opera-buffa.

The dramatic poet of the day in Vienna was Marco Cottellini. He had written libretti for Gassmann, Hasse, and Salieri, and for Mozart he now wrote "La Finta Semplice." Wolfgang instantly set to work, for he and his father hoped that the opera might be given by Easter. Meanwhile the work progressed more slowly than he had counted upon. The librettist caused delays by frequent alterations in the text. Still Wolfgang spared no pains, and had soon completed a considerable score of six hundred and fourteen pages. For the overture a symphony was chosen which Mozart had composed on the 16th of January, soon after his return from Ollmuetz to Vienna. It was now that the intrigues began against the representation of the work. It was even asserted that the opera was not composed by Wolfgang, but by his father, and Leopold found it necessary to resort to drastic measures to refute this suggestion of envy. In the presence of Prince Kaunitz, the Duke of Braganza, Metastasio, and Hasse, and a distinguished company, Leopold caused the first volume of Metastasio's works which came to hand to be opened, and the first aria which presented itself to be placed before Wolfgang. "He seized the pen, and wrote, without hesitation, in the presence of many persons of distinction, the music to the aria for several instruments with the most astonishing swiftness," writes Leopold. But the struggle against Wolfgang grew more bitter; the performers, too, were insincere, and Affligio began to entertain doubts as to the result.

Affligio had begun life as an adventurer and gambler, then became an impresario, and ended his career on the galleys. He was Mozart's first impresario. He postponed the performance of the opera from Easter to Whitsuntide, then to the return of the Emperor from Hungary. "Now you will wonder," writes Leopold, "why Prince Kaunitz and other grand people, or even the Emperor himself, do not order the opera to be performed." The explanation lay, according to him, in the fact that Affligio had engaged French comedians at a yearly cost of over seventy thousand florins, which the Emperor could not be prevailed upon to pay, as Prince Kaunitz, behind the Emperor's back, had promised Affligio he should. So that for fear of the seventy thousand florins, no one would speak to Affligio with authority and decision. Meanwhile enemies in Salzburg had circulated the report that Wolfgang had received two thousand florins for his opera. Two months before—it was now about the end of July—the archbishop had sent word to Leopold that he had nothing to say against extending his leave, but that during his absence from Salzburg he should pay him no salary. Thus misfortunes accumulated; and when Affligio declared to Leopold that he would willingly give the opera, only he feared it might be hissed off the stage, there was no other course open to the Mozarts than an honourable retreat.

On the 21st of September, Leopold presented a complaint against Affligio to the Emperor. The court musical director, Count Spork, was commissioned to inquire into the matter, and Affligio received a summons to answer the charge. But all was in vain; the opera was not given. Undeceived at last, Leopold began to turn his thoughts to Italy, especially Florence and Naples, as a means of compensation for Wolfgang. On the 7th of December the consecration of a church for the orphan asylum, newly organized by Father Parhammer, took place in presence of the imperial court. Wolfgang had received a commission to write a mass and a few sacred pieces for the occasion, among them a trumpet concerto, which one of the orphan boys was to play. This last-named piece is not in existence, but the mass, the first which Mozart wrote, has been preserved. In this branch of music the boy felt, and intelligibly so, least sure of himself; for the traditional form of this kind of composition was very strictly and closely defined. Besides Wolfgang, lately busy with a cheerful opera, could scarcely have felt real pleasure in sacred composition. However, the performance of the mass had the effect of convincing all the world of the malice of Mozart's adversaries. Mozart remembered, even in later life, the solemn impression he received when, for the first time in public. he wielded the conductor's bâton.

As to the artistic value of the opera which was not performed in Vienna, "La Finta Semplice," the score, which is still extant, proves that it not only stands high among the comic operas of that time, but even surpasses them. It has been already mentioned that Mozart introduced into it one of the arias for tenor out of his first oratorio. Mozart's first German opera was performed at the private theatre of Dr. Anton Meszmer, a rich citizen of Vienna. It was called "Bastien und Bastienne," and the libretto was an imitation of Madame Favart's parody of Rousseau's "Devin du Villag"." In the music Mozart preserves the pastoral character; he has also introduced an imitation of the bagpipes, and indulges in the joke of mimicking certain sounds produced by the wind instruments when played without artistic skill. He had made use of such clever tricks in art previously, as we have seen in the "Galimathias," composed at the Hague for the Prince of Orange. The style in this first attempt of Mozart's at German opera is remarkably different; he follows closely in the steps of J. A. Hiller's German operettas. It is interesting, too, to observe that the arias have no *da capo* after their second part, as the form of the Italian aria prescribes. But, above all, we are struck with admiration for this boy of twelve years old, who was equally at home in Italian opera-buffa, with its traditional and strictly-defined limits, and in this German opera, his own independent venture, developed by him with such certainty and aptitude. A popular Vienna journal of the year 1768, prints an air from "Bastien," with the words "Dafne, deine Rosenwangen," and another song of Wolfgang's, "Freude Königin der Weisen"—a proof that his popularity was already firmly established and on the increase.

With disappointed hopes the family returned to Salzburg towards the end of December, 1768. In the following year the archbishop tried to make up to the Mozarts for their disappointment at Vienna. He had "Lι Finta Semplice" performed, and Wolfgang received a further mark of distinction by being appointed concertmeister. The year 1769 was spent by the new concertmeister in his studies at Salzburg. The few compositions of this year indicate the nature of these studies, in particular, two masses, which prove that Leopold Mozart educated his son in a strict school.

Meanwhile the project of a journey to Italy was approaching fulfilment. In the last century Italy was the musician's Eldorado. To study there, to win his first laurels there, was the ambition of every aspirant for musical fame. Leopold Mozart's chief object in view was to remove his son from his narrow provincial surroundings at Salzburg. His attempt at Vienna in the previous year having been unsuccessful, Italy seemed now to be naturally the next place in which to repeat the experiment. Concerning this memorable tour we have the interesting accounts contained in the letters of Leopold and of Wolfgang Mozart. Wolfgang's letters mostly breathe a natural, cheerful, and child-like spirit; he indulges in all manner of little jokes with his sister, to whom his correspondence is chiefly addressed. Only if music is his theme, his tone becomes more earnest; his frankness vies with the goodnature and amiability he always displays in describing his exciting musical adventures. In the beginning of December, 1769, father and son started on their journey. Their first halting-place was Innsbruck, where they were well received by Count Spaur, brother to the Dean of Salzburg. On the 14th of December, in an "academy" (concert) presided over by Count Künigl, Mozart played at sight a new concerto which was laid before him. He received the concerto as a present, and besides a reward of twelve ducats. At Roveredo Leopold Mozart came across an old pupil, the Kreishauptmann Christani. Christani observed that Wolfgang greatly resembled his mother, whom he could well remember. They also met with other old acquaintances. At this place a concert was arranged for them by the nobility, to take place at the house of Baron Todeschi. When on the day of the concert Wolfgang wanted to play the organ in the church, he and his father on arriving found it so crowded, that it was only by dint of much assistance that they could make their way to the organ.

The new year, 1770, found the travellers at Verona. Here they had to wait a week before the nobility could get up a concert, on account of the opera. Wolfgang had a symphony played before an assembly of connoisseurs, and an aria composed to a given text, which he himself sang, and improvised on given themes. At the church of St. Tommaso the scenes of Roveredo were repeated. At the order of the comptroller-general, Lugiati, a life-size picture of Wolfgang was painted, for which he sat twice, on the 7th and 8th of January. "La dolce sua effigie mi è di conforto ed altresi di eccitamento a riprendere qualche fiata la musica," writes Leopold to his wife. Mozart is seated somewhat to the left in the picture, in a carved armchair. He is playing on the harpsichord, his youthful, cheerful countenance turned towards the spectator. He wears a red gold-embroidered coat, and on the little finger of the right hand a diamond ring. The words "Molto Allegro G major $\frac{3}{4}$" are clearly visible on the open music-book. Lugiati himself wrote to Frau Mozart about the "raro e portentoso giovane." The winter of 1769-70 was by no means an Italian one, and the Mozarts suffered much from the cold. On the 10th of January they arrived in Mantua, where they also met with much politeness from distinguished amateurs. Fashionable ladies overwhelmed Wolfgang with attentions and costly gifts. On the 16th of January there was a concert of the Philharmonic Society, to which Wolfgang actively contributed. Of the sixteen numbers which the concert comprised, there were nine in which he took part. The result was brilliant. The musicians said that this boy seemed born to put to shame experienced masters of the art.

Towards the end of January we find father and son again in Milan, and dwelling with the Augustine fathers of St. Marco.

Their life there, as Leopold Mozart expressly states, was not "free," but comfortable and safe. Moreover, they were near to Count Carl Joseph Firmian, the Governor-General of Milan, who was a warm and sincere patron of Mozart. The count had begun his studies at Salzburg, where his elder brother was archbishop, till 1740, but, on account of his liberal tendencies, had been sent away shortly afterwards to Leyden, there to continue his education. He had since travelled through Italy and France, and was altogether a man of great cultivation. The celebrated Winckelmann, who had made his acquaintance when the count was Austrian ambassador at Naples, looked upon him as one of the greatest, and most learned men of his time. As Governor-General he stood at the head of the first society in Milan, to which he introduced both the Mozarts. Father and son entered into all the amusements of the carnival, but were prudent enough to take care of their health, so that Leopold could satisfy his wife's motherly anxiety about Wolfgang with a clear conscience. He writes: "I can assure you that I have never yet seen him so careful of his health as in this country. Whatever does not seem good for him he lets alone, and many days he eats very little, but he is fat and well and gay and happy all day long." They had to conform to the Milanese carnival costume, which consisted of a cloak and hood covering the head up to the chin, and falling down over the shoulders. The dress was remarkably becoming to Wolfgang, as Leopold relates, while the careful father of a family adds, "As we have been obliged to go to this foolish expense, I comfort myself with the reflection that we can use it for all sorts of other things, and at least it will come in for coat-linings, neckties, &c."

At the opera Piccini was at that time in vogue, and Mozart praises his "Cesare in Egitto." The Mozarts became personally acquainted with Piccini and his wife. Wolfgang's performances were admired on all sides. The musicians, too, among them Giambattista Sammartini, who, at the time, had a great reputation in Milan, meted out applause to him with no niggard hand. But the young artist's best friend was Count Firmian. On the 12th of March he presented the youthful *maestro* to a brilliant assembly, headed by the Duke of Modena, with the princess and the cardinal-archbishop. For this occasion Wolfgang had composed three arias from Metastasio, in order to prove that he had perfect command of the serious dramatic style. His success was brilliant in the extreme. He received from the count a snuff-box containing twenty ducats, and a beautiful edition of Metastasio's works. It was then and there decided that he was to write the next opera, provided permission could be obtained from the Archbishop of Salzburg, who was immediately written to on the subject. The libretto was to be sent after the young *maestro*, who was travelling next to Rome and Naples. An honorarium of a hundred ducats (*gigliati*), was settled upon, with lodgings free during his residence in Milan. By November the opera was to be ready, and then to be put on the stage as speedily as possible. Furnished by Count Firmian with numerous letters of introduction, on the 15th of March the Mozarts travelled as far as Lodi, where Wolfgang composed the same evening, at seven o'clock, just after arriving, his first string quartet. At Parma they met with a friendly reception from the singer Lucrezia Agujari, called "La Bastardella," who possessed a voice of almost incredible compass. Wolfgang has noted in his letters a string of passages which she sang to him. In it the high C (*ut acuto*) occurs. Leopold confirms this, and adds, "She has, besides, an excellent contralto range down to G. She is not handsome, but neither is she ugly, has at times a wild look in her eyes like people who are subject to convulsions, and limps with one foot. Otherwise she is of good conduct, and therefore has a good character and a good name." To make the acquaintance of such stars of song was by no means unimportant for young Mozart.

On the 24th of March the travellers entered Bologna. Field-Marshal Count Pallavicini got up in honour of them an "academy" in his house, at which a hundred and fifty persons of the nobility, with the Roman cardinal-legate, Antonio Colonna Branciforte, at their head, were present, whilst among the connoisseurs was the celebrated Padre Martini. The concert began at half-past seven, and was not over till midnight. Besides Wolfgang, the singers Aprili and Cicognani assisted at it. Leopold expresses his delight at their extraordinary popularity in Bologna, and in the fact that Wolfgang was more admired here than in any other town of Italy, "for it is the dwelling-place of many masters, artists, and learned men." "Here," he continues, "he has been put to the severest test, and this increases his fame throughout Italy, for the Padre Martini is the idol of the Italians, and he speaks of Wolfgang with much admiration, and makes him submit to every test." The Padre Martini was undoubtedly the first musical authority of the day; he was looked upon as an oracle in all important musical questions, and not in Italy alone. Dr. Burney devoted special attention to him in his travels. To be commended by Padre Martini was a guarantee of an auspicious future. We can therefore understand how Leopold rejoiced as the Padre again and again expressed himself pleased with each new fugue that he made Wolfgang compose on a given theme. It was a great thing for the travellers, as regards Wolfgang's acquaintance with the peculiarities and exigencies of the art of singing, that they were favourably received by the celebrated singer Farinelli (Carlo Broschi), a pupil of Porpora. Farinelli, loaded in the course of time with honours and riches, was resting on his laurels, and dwelt on a beautiful estate in the neighbourhood of Bologna. Burney, too, had the good fortune to hear Farinelli sing. Wolfgang was able to improve in his singing; it is significant that here, when a boy, he should have had the opportunity of perceiving for himself the power and difficulty of vocal art. Curiosity, too, kept the travellers some time at Bologna, and the collections at the "Istituto" prompted Leopold to an interesting comparison with the British Museum.

On the 30th of March father and son entered Florence, where, through the good offices of the Austrian ambassador, Count Rosenberg, they were introduced to the Grand Duke Leopold, who recollected their meeting in Vienna, and even asked after "Nannerl" (Marianne). On the 2nd of April Wolfgang played at court, accompanied by the renowned violinist Nardini and the director of music at the grand ducal court, the Marchese di Ligniville. The latter put before Wolfgang a fugue to play, and gave him the most difficult themes to treat. "Wolfgang played, and did it all as one eats a piece of bread." The Marchese di Ligniville was accounted one of the most thorough of Italian contrapuntists. Wolfgang learned many of the canons which occur in the Marchese's "Stabat Mater" for three voices. At Florence the Mozarts met an old London acquaintance, the singer Manzuoli. A very intimate friendship grew up here between Wolfgang and a young Englishman of the same age, Thomas Linley, born at Bath in 1756, who was studying the violin with Nardini, and had already attained so much excellence that he was considered equal to his teacher. The two boys were so fond of each other that they never separated without tears. Burney, who was travelling in Italy about this time, says that throughout Italy people spoke of Tommasino and little Mozart as two geniuses destined to fulfil the greatest expectations. Thomas Linley was drowned when quite a young man, in 1778, during an excursion on the water. The singer Kelly relates how Wolfgang grieved when he heard the news afterwards in Vienna.

Meanwhile, delightful as Florence was to them, and to Leopold particularly, the Mozarts had to say farewell to the beautiful city, in order to reach Rome in time for the musical solemnities of Passion week at the Sistine Chapel. After a journey signalized by the worst possible weather, they entered Rome on Wednesday in Passion week amidst a storm of thunder and lightning, "received like great men with the firing of heavy guns." They went straight to the Sistine Chapel to hear the famous "Miserere" of Allegri, which was held in such esteem that the musicians of the chapel were forbidden, on pain of excommunication, to take home or to copy any portion of it out of the chapel. "But we have it all the same," writes Leopold triumphantly. Wolfgang had written it out from memory, and at its repetition on Good Friday corrected those passages in which his memory had failed him. This feat became known, and excited the wonder and admiration of the Papal singer Christofori. People in Salzburg said that Wolfgang had committed a sin. Leopold therefore positively wrote, "All Rome knows it, and even the Pope is aware that Wolfgang has written out the 'Miserere.' There is no cause for apprehension. It has brought him honour. You must absolutely have the letter read everywhere, and make it known to his Princely Highness the Archbishop." With peculiar satisfaction Leopold relates how politely every one made room for them, and how Wolfgang was treated as a German prince, and himself as his tutor. At the cardinals' table Wolfgang was placed close to the seat of Cardinal Pallavicini, who, after looking attentively at the boy's intelligent countenance, nodded to him, and said, "Will you be so good as to tell me in confidence who you are?" Wolfgang told him. The cardinal replied in great astonishment, "What! are you the famous boy of whom so much has been written to me?" Thereupon Wolfgang asked, "Are you not Cardinal Pallavicini?" The cardinal answered, "I am. Why?" Wolfgang then told him that his father had letters of introduction to his Eminence, and that they would wait upon him. The cardinal expressed great pleasure at this. He said that Wolfgang spoke good Italian, and added, "Ick kan auk ein benig deutsch sprekken." It is interesting that in the midst of so many new impressions, which must to some extent have deeply engaged his attention, Wolfgang still thought so much of home that he sent thither a newly composed country-dance, and made his father write how he wished he could step to it. At the request of a Herr von Mœlck, from Salzburg, who was studying at the "Collegio dell' Anima," Wolfgang played them a few of his own compositions.

It was not without apprehension, on account of the insecurity of travelling by the so-called Procaccio-carriage – a sort of diligence—that the Mozarts on the 8th of May began the journey from Rome to Naples. They were glad to find companions in four Augustine friars, whose good offices procured them a hospitable reception at the convents lying on the route. On the 13th of May they were present at Capua at the ceremony of the taking of the veil by a nun of rank. "Excepting the nearest relatives, no one was invited to the midday repast at the nunnery but ourselves." The Mozarts obtained an introduction to the court of Naples through the mediation of the all-powerful minister Tanucci. Queen Caroline was very friendly, but there was no playing at court, for the king took no interest in music. Tanucci placed his major-domo at the disposal of the travellers, whereupon the whole of the nobility vied with each other in their attentions to the Mozarts. Very kindly disposed towards them was Metastasio's protectress, the old Princess Belmonti. They met with rare hospitality too from the English ambassador, Sir William Hamilton, who had made their acquaintance in London. Sir William's first wife was held to be the finest performer on the harpsichord in Naples. Burney and Kelly both praise her pathetic and expressive playing. But she trembled when about to play before Wolfgang. Other old friends whom the Mozarts met here were the Swiss Tschudy and Mörikofer and the Dutchman Doncker. On the 28th of May they gave a concert, which was brilliantly attended, and which brought them in rich profits. When Wolfgang played at the Conservatorio della Pietà, the agility of his left hand roused the audience to great excitement. They declared that there was witchcraft in his ring, and it was only upon his drawing it off that they became quiet again, and admired his execution anew.

The opera began at San Carlo on the 30th of May with a distinguished list of performers; amongst them the Amicis and the singer Aprili. The operas of Jomelli, who in 1768 had left Stuttgard and settled in Naples, met with no applause. In Wolfgang's opinion the "Armida abbandonata" was a fine work, but too learned and too old-fashioned for the theatre. Before they left, an offer was made to Wolfgang to write an opera for San Carlo, which, however, he was obliged to decline, as he was already bound to write one for Milan. After witnessing an eruption of Vesuvius, and therewith the greatest wonder of Naples, the Mozarts travelled post to Rome in twenty-seven hours. In the last stage, owing to the brutal lashing of the horses by the postilion, one of them became frightened and upset the carriage. Leopold was wounded on the shin in trying to protect his son. The wound, though not dangerous, was severe, and he was obliged to keep his bed some days. Wolfgang, too, was so tired out that on his arrival in Rome he went fast asleep on a chair, and his father had to put him to bed asleep as he was. When he awoke the next morning at nine o'clock, he had no idea where he was, nor how he had got into bed. At Rome they had the opportunity of seeing and admiring the famous girandola, the lighting up of the dome of St. Peter's, and other splendours. They had an audience of the Pope on the 8th of July, when his Holiness bestowed upon Wolfgang the Cross of the Order of the Golden Spur, "the same that Gluck has, and which is called 'Te creamus auratæ militiæ equitem.' He has to wear a beautiful golden cross, and you can picture to yourself how I laugh every time I hear him called Signor Cavaliere," writes the happy father. During the next year he insisted upon putting on the title-pages of compositions "Del Sign. Cavaliere W. A. Mozart." Wolfgang only wore the cross on his visit to Paris; afterwards he thought no more about it, and we never hear of "Ritter Mozart." It is one of the finest traits in the character of the great musician that he cared nothing for external marks of distinction. Outwardly and inwardly his art was to him the badge of honour he most prized. Before the Mozarts left Rome, Pompeo Battoni painted a life-size portrait of the young master. The picture, one of the finest of Mozart, came to England in the possession of Mr. Haydon. Some time ago it was placed in the Kensington Museum by its then owner, John Ella. An engraving, executed by Adlard, which appeared in "Records of the Musical Union, 1865," is a faithful reproduction of the original. The picture has lately been sold. On the 10th of July the Mozarts left Rome, and, travelling by way of Civita Castellana, Loretto, and Sinigaglia, reached Bologna on the 20th, where they purposed to remain until Wolfgang's presence in Milan for the *stagione* (season) should be required.

Wolfgang had gained much in height while in Naples. He now began to grow so fast that his father declared he would be nearly grown up by the time he reached home. The injured leg still gave Leopold much trouble, and he complains more than once of the increased expense it caused him. An invitation, therefore, from Count Pallavicini to spend the hot season at a country-seat, rented by him in the neighbourhood of Bologna, was very welcome. On the 27th of July the libretto for the new opera, with the names of the singers, arrived. The title of the opera was "Mitridate, Re di Ponto," and the author, Vittorio Amadeo Cigna-Santi, a poet of Turin, where the work, with music by Quirino Gasparini, had already been represented. The chief performers were to be the tenor Ettore, the prima donna Antonia Bernasconi, and the soprano Santorini.

In the beginning of August the Mozarts went to the count's country seat, "Alla croce del Biacco." The young Count Pallavicini became Wolfgang's greatest friend. At this time Leopold's health was a source of anxiety to the whole family. The receipt of a letter from Wolfgang bearing testimony to his well-being must, therefore, have been a great satisfaction to them. He says: "I am still alive, and very jolly indeed. To-day I had the pleasure of riding on a donkey. For in Italy this is the custom, and so I thought I must at any rate try it too. We have the honour to associate with a certain Dominican, who is looked upon as a saint. I, indeed, do not quite believe in it, for he often takes for breakfast a cup of chocolate, and directly after that a good glass of strong Spanish wine, and I have even had the honour to dine with this saint, and he took his wine at table like a man, and at the last a whole glassful of strong wine, two good slices of melon, peaches, pears, five cups of coffee, a whole plateful of cloves, and two platefuls of milk and lemons. This, however, he may have done on purpose, though I believe not, for it would be too much, but he takes many things in the afternoon." These are Wolfgang's childish impressions; his father writes further that the Dominican "is a German-Bohemian." Of Wolfgang he says: "Everything is too small for him; all his limbs have grown bigger and stronger. He has no voice for singing. It is completely gone; he has neither high notes nor low, and not five pure tones. This is very vexing to him, for he cannot sing his own things, which he would often like to do," so that towards the end of August, 1770, Wolfgang's voice was beginning to break.

On the 30th of this month they heard in Bologna the high mass and vespers of the "Academia filarmonica," which were composed by ten different masters. Burney was also present at this solemnity, and expressly mentions in his journal that the Mozarts were there, father and son. The society resolved to admit Wolfgang in accordance with his supplication, as "compositore." Leopold writes: "He had to appear in the hall of the Academy at four o'clock in the afternoon of the 9th of October. There the 'Princeps Academiæ,' and the two censors, all of whom are old capellmeisters, gave him, in presence of all the members, an Antiphon from the Antiphonarium, which he had to set for four voices in an adjoining room to which he was led by the beadle, who shut the door. When he had done, it was examined by the censors and all the capellmeisters and composers, and put to the vote by means of black and white balls. As all the balls were white, he was called. On his entrance they all clapped their hands, and after the 'Princeps' in the name of the society had declared him elected, they wished him good luck. He returned thanks, and then it was over. Meanwhile I and my companion were shut up on the other side of the hall in the library of the Academy. Every one was astonished that he had done it so quickly, for many had spent three hours over an Antiphon of three lines. N.B. You must know, however, that it is not easy, for this kind of composition excludes many things which one may not use in it, and this he had been told beforehand. He did it in a good half-hour. The beadle brought us the diploma to our house. Among others these words are in it:—'Testamur Dominum W. A. Mozart inter Academiæ nostræ Magistros Compositores adscriptum fuisse.' It does him all the more honour, as the Academy is more than a hundred years old, and besides, Padre Martini and other Italians of note, distinguished men of other nations are members of the Academia bononiensis." Wolfgang had practised the particular form of composition spoken of under the guidance of Padre Martini. The original of his "trial-piece" has been published by Gaspari in his book "La Musica in Bologna." In the Mozarteum at Salzburg there is a second version of the same Antiphon in Wolfgang's hand, which, in all likelihood, is an exercise set him by Padre Martini after the first piece. The chief advantage of Wolfgang's election was that he could call himself, with perfect justice, an "Academico filarmonico."

On the 18th of October the travellers entered Milan, where the opera "Mitridate" was energetically commenced. Wolfgang had begun the recitatives at Bologna. The more important portions of the music had in a manner to be completed with the assistance of the singers concerned, for upon them depended almost entirely the success of the opera. Unfortunately the singers were very late in arriving at Milan, and but little time remained to Wolfgang for composing. A greater seriousness is observable in his letters of this time. He writes to his mother on the 20th of October: "I cannot work much, for my fingers ache with writing so much recitative. I beg mamma to pray for me, that it may go well with the opera, and that we may be happy again together." He also asks "his heart's little sister Marianne" to pray to God that the opera may go well. Leopold was anxious not to overtask Wolfgang's strength. He never allowed him to write after dinner, but took him out for a walk. Wolfgang generally had plenty of self-confidence. "With God's help we shall fight our way successfully through the unavoidable vexations which every capellmeister must endure from the virtuoso canaille."

It was lucky for the Mozarts that instead of the prima donna originally chosen—Gabrielli—Antonia Bernasconi, a native of Würtemberg, was fixed upon. Aided by her "the first battle" was happily fought. An unknown adversary of Wolfgang tried to persuade her to send back his arias, and in their stead to study the compositions of Gasparini, which he had brought her. "But she refused this wicked man," writes Leopold, "and she is quite beside herself with delight over the arias which Wolfgang has written for her according to her will and pleasure. So, too, is her master Lampugnani, who goes through her part with her, and who cannot have enough of Wolfgang's arias." Another storm was looming in the theatrical sky, roused by the tenor, Cavaliere Guglielmo d'Ettore. The particulars are not known, but it must have been serious, for Leopold reminds his son of it during his visit to Paris. Santorini, the soprano, did not arrive till the 1st of December, and the first representation of the opera was fixed for the 26th. But, on the other hand, much went on prosperously. The copyist did his work so well, that at the rehearsal only one mistake was found in the recitatives. "I only wish it may be as well with the copy of the instrumental parts," writes Leopold." "As far as I can say without fatherly partiality, it seems to me that Wolfgang has written the opera well, and with much spirit. The singers are good. It is only a question now of the orchestra, and lastly of the caprice of the audience. Consequently much depends on good luck, just as in a lottery."

The orchestra numbered some sixty performers, among them fourteen first, and an equal number of second, violins. At first there was no lack of persons to cry out that it was impossible so young a boy—a German too—could write an Italian opera, or that he could make use of the chiaroscuro indispensable in dramatic music. But, after the first rehearsal, these voices were silenced. The singers—men and women—were full of confidence. The instrumentalists praised the music, and said it was bright, clear, and easy to play. Sammartini, too, declared himself in favour of the music.

On the 26th of December, the day appointed, the first representation of the opera, at which Wolfgang conducted, took place. The whole audience shouted " Evviva il Maestro ! Evviva il Maestrino !" Contrary to all custom, at this first performance an aria of the prima donna was encored, and at the second, on the 27th of December, two of her arias had to be repeated. "Just as Hasse was called ' il Sassone,' Galuppi ' il Buranello,' so our son is called ' il Cava-

liere filarmonico,'" Leopold writes home to his wife. With
the addition of the ballets, each performance lasted a good six
hours, so that it was desirable to be cautious in the matter
of encores. The enthusiasm increased with every representation. The Milan Gazette of the 2nd of January, 1771, said:
" The opera has obtained the approbation of the public, no
less through the good taste with which it has been put upon
the stage, than through the excellence of the music and the
art of the performers. Several of the arias for the prima
donna express the emotions in a most lively manner, and stir
the soul. The young capellmeister, who is not yet fifteen
years of age, has studied the beautiful in nature, and decked
it with rare musical charms." This critique confirms Leopold's report: " As the Italians say, the new opera is
' dalle stelle' (from the stars)." The opera was given twenty
times to full houses. Of the further fate of "Mitridate"
we learn that the copyist obtained commissions for five complete scores—two for Vienna, one for the Duchess of Parma,
one for the manager of the theatre, and one for the Court of
Lisbon.

On the 5th of January, 1771, the "Academica filarmonica" of Verona received Wolfgang as capellmeister among
its members. The same day he gave an "Academy" at the
house of Count Firmian. Soon afterwards an excursion was
made to Turin, and then the return journey, of which Venice
was to be the next stage, began. The Mozarts reached Venice
on Carnival Monday. Here they found a magnificent reception at the house of the merchant Wider, a business corre-
spondent of Hagenauer of Salzburg, whose son John had
been placed with this family. On the 5th of March the
Mozarts gave a grand "Academy." The noble society of
Venice were so delighted with the young maestro that they
would hardly let him go away. At last, however, the Mozarts set out. At Padua Wolfgang received a commission to
compose an oratorio, probably " La Betulia liberata." At
Vicenza the travellers stayed a few days with the Bishop
Cornero, and at Verona with their friend Luggiati. An
agreement was concluded about this time with the management of Milan for the first opera of the Carnival of 1773,
which Wolfgang was to write for a hundred and thirty
gigliati (ducats). On the 28th of March, 1771, the travellers

reached Salzburg once more. A few days after, Wolfgang received a letter from Count Firmian commissioning him, in the name of the Empress Maria Theresa, to write a dramatic serenata for the marriage of the Archduke Ferdinand with the Princess Maria of Modena, which was to take place at Milan on the 15th of October, 1771.

On this account the Mozarts could only remain a short time in Salzburg. Wolfgang was certainly the archbishop's concertmeister, but for this he received no pay. Still, in order to do something in his official capacity, he composed during the summer a litany, a "regina cœli," and a symphony. Leopold Mozart was anxious to strengthen his son's position in Salzburg, whilst doubtful if it would prove of long duration. For the young Mozart did not trouble himself much about little politenesses and civilities. During this visit to his native town, Wolfgang fell in love for the first time. The lady of his heart was older than he, and shortly to be married, but this did not hinder him from pouring out passionate declarations concerning his love-affair, in his letters to his sister. These letters were written on the journey begun by father and son on the 13th of August. After a short stay with their friend Luggiati at Verona, they arrived in Milan on the 21st of August. The libretto of the serenata was still at Vienna on approval. This circumstance, however, did not at all disturb Wolfgang's serene temper. The young composer was very graciously received by the bride, the Princess Maria. When the book arrived, about the end of August, the author, Giuseppe Parini, still had some things to alter in it, so that Wolfgang could not get it in hand till September. He set to work on it, however, with such zeal that the recitatives and choruses were finished by the 13th. In another twelve days, as his father predicted, the serenata was completed. Such speed excited great astonishment, especially in the house in which the Mozarts lived, for overhead was a violinist, and beneath a second violin, while next to them a singing-master gave lessons, and opposite lived an oboist. "It is nice to compose, it gives one much to think," Wolfgang writes home.

With the artists who were to assist in the performance they had very pleasant relations; these were Caterina Gabrielli, the tenor Sibaldi, and the soprano Manzuoli. The latter they had met before in London. Hasse too, who composed the festival opera, Metastasio's "Ruggiero," was very friendly; he also had previously patronized young Mozart. It is remarkable that this man, who had long exclusively ruled the Italian stage, should have so ungrudgingly given place to a young boy. After listening to the serenata, he exclaimed, "The youth will outshine us all." On the 15th of October the festivities began with the solemn entry of the Archduke; immediately afterwards his wedding with the Princess of Modena took place in the cathedral. Next followed a concert and kissing of hands at court. On the 16th there was a grand banquet, to which four hundred couples, all portioned by Maria Theresa, sat down. In the evening, Hasse's "Ruggiero" with two ballets was given. On the 17th, after a grand "corso" Wolfgang's serenata "Ascanio in Alba," an allegorical pastoral, with choruses and dances by Favier, was performed; Leopold Mozart had foreseen its great success. The applause was extraordinary. The serenata had to be repeated next day, and Leopold could say with justice, "I am sorry Wolfgang's serenata has put Hasse's opera in the shade, so much so that I cannot describe it." This statement is confirmed and made complete by the account of a young man—Kerschbaumer—the son of a Salzburg merchant, who was present at the second performance on the 24th of October, and to whom Leopold refers the family at Salzburg. Besides the price agreed on, Wolfgang received from the Empress a gold watch set with diamonds, and ornamented with the portrait of Maria Theresa. During the festivities, a stand erected for spectators fell, killing and injuring more than fifty persons. By a mere chance Leopold Mozart and his son had obtained places in the court balcony; otherwise they would have been on the stand, and shared in the danger. Before leaving Milan, an agreement was entered into with regard to the second carnival opera of 1773, for the San Benedetto theatre at Venice. But the contract never came to fulfilment, for Naumann stepped into Wolfgang's place, and made a great success with his "Soliman." The return of the Mozarts to Salzburg was delayed until the middle of December. On the 30th Wolfgang composed a symphony.

The new year, 1772, began for Wolfgang with a severe illness, from which, however, he soon recovered. The

Mozarts had scarcely returned to Salzburg, when on the 16th of December, 1771, the Archbishop Sigismund died. On the 14th of March, 1772, Hieronymus Josef Franz von Paola, Count Colloredo, hitherto Bishop of Gurk, was appointed to the vacant see, much to the astonishment and grief of the people, who had expected that Count Ferdinand von Zeil, subsequently bishop of Chiemsee, would be chosen. An eye-witness gives an account of the first impression made by the choice in the following words:—" When the solemn procession of the chapter, the pale, feeble, and newly appointed bishop in its midst, began the Te Deum a sullen silence reigned. It was fair time. A street-boy cheered amidst the gazing, silent crowd. But a strange merchant standing by gave him a box on the ear, with the words: 'Boy, you cheer while the people weep.'" So little beloved was the future ruler of Salzburg. With this man the Mozarts were to have many conflicts.

For the festivities in connexion with the installation of the new archbishop, an opera was to be performed. The subject chosen was Metastasio's "Sogno di Scipione," an allegorical *azione teatrale* which had been written forty years before for the Imperial court, and dealt with the unfortunate events of the war in Italy. The bravery and resolution of a certain general, which did not desert him in the hour of misfortune, were dwelt upon and magnified. Whether this subject-matter might be appropriate or not seems scarcely to have been considered. Wolfgang was commissioned to compose the music, and naturally acquitted himself in such a manner that the result was a fine opera, in which, however, the heart and genuine feeling had no voice. On the 24th of October, father and son again set out on a journey to Milan. On the way they made a short stay at Botzen, at Ala with the brothers Piccinni, and at Verona with Luggiati. When they reached Milan on the 4th of November, Leopold Mozart was unwell. He was suffering from pain in the head consequent upon an accident, and became a prey to gloomy thoughts, which may well have been the reflection of the evil days he had fallen upon, under the new archbishop. Moreover the desire of his heart—to see Wolfgang in an established position— was still unfulfilled. The opera with which Wolfgang was now entrusted, was "Lucio Silla" by Giovanni de Gamera. The recitatives he had brought with him all ready. But

E

alterations in the text became necessary, and so a part of the recitatives had to be composed anew. As the singers were not yet in Milan, he had time enough. One by one they arrived; Signora Felicita Suarti first, then the soprano Rauz- zini, a performer on the harpsichord and a not unimportant composer as well ; then, on the 4th of December, the prima donna Maria Anne de Amicis, a pupil of Tesi, and afterwards of Christopher Bach in London. Of her Leopold Mozart observes after the rehearsals : " She sings like an angel. The whole of Salzburg would be amazed to hear anything like it." The tenor Cardoni was finally announced to be seriously ill. His place had to be filled by a church singer from Lodi, Bassano Morgnoni, a man who had never yet sung on a large stage. In the meanwhile the chief rehearsal went off well, and although, at the first representation, there were not want- ing various little misunderstandings which created some amuse- ment, the opera won immediate approval, and the applause increased with every performance. It was given more than twenty times, and each time to a full house. Some of the arias had always to be repeated.

At the beginning of 1773, Wolfgang composed for Rauzzini a motet, which the latter sang on the 15th of January at the Theatine monastery. Later Leopold Mozart relates that Wolfgang is busy with a quartet. Their departure from Milan was constantly postponed by Leopold. He had good reasons for the delay. For with recommendations from Count Firmian he had sent his son's new opera to the Grand Duke Leopold of Tuscany, and at the same time a petition for Wolfgang's appointment at the Florentine court. But the negotiation had no favourable result, and it became evident to Leopold that they must attempt a new tour. "Spend as little as possible," he writes to the family at Salzburg ; "for money we must have, if we are to undertake a journey; I grudge every kreutzer which we spend in Salzburg." At last they had to leave Milan in order to be at Salzburg for the anniversary of the archbishop's installation. Probably the latter had refused to prolong their leave of absence. In the summer of this year, 1773, the archbishop went to Vienna. Leopold Mozart took the opportunity of his master's absence to go there himself with his son. Arrived at Vienna they presented themselves before the archbishop, who gave them permission to remain away some time longer, as he himself was not yet thinking of returning. The real object of this visit to Vienna remains unknown. Meanwhile it is certain that one of its results was to procure for Wolfgang a better position. The Mozarts had an audience of the Empress, who received them most graciously. Old friends were delighted to see them again, and especially the Meszmer family, at whose private theatre Wolfgang had brought out " Bastien und Bastienne." Whilst they were in Vienna, the order of the Jesuits was abolished. Wolfgang composed at this time a serenade and a quartet for strings. At the Theatine monastery he played on the violin. The organ there was so bad that he could not play a concerto upon it. But there was no opportunity of earning money. So much the more welcome, therefore, was the commission to compose an opera-buffa for the carnival of 1775 at Munich. Wolfgang owed this invitation apparently to his old patron, Count Ferdinand von Zeil, prince-bishop of Chiemsee. The Elector Maximilian III. of Bavaria had been interested in Mozart when a boy. Yet the Archbishop Hieronymus took great credit to himself for placing his concertmeister at the disposal of the Elector. The sister of the Elector was the widowed Electress of Saxony, Maria Antonia Walburga, called Talea Ernelinda in her capacity of " pastorella Arcada." She was at this time in Munich, where a lively musical intercourse soon commenced. The Electress Walburga was herself a singer and composer. We are acquainted with one of her works, the opera " Talestri Regina delle Amazone."

The Mozarts remained quietly in Salzburg from the end of September, 1773, till late in the autumn of 1774. During this time Wolfgang composed a number of works. The list includes two masses, a litany, several symphonies, two serenades, a divertimento, a quintet for string instruments, and the first concerto for the harpsichord attempted by him since childhood. On the 6th of December he travelled with his father to Munich, where they were found pleasant quarters in the house of Canon Joseph von Pernat. Wolfgang was suffering from neuralgic toothache, brought on by the intense cold of the journey, and for the first week his swollen cheeks obliged him to keep his room. He was subject to this complaint, and at times suffered much from it. The opera which brought the Mozarts to Munich was "La Finta Giardiniera." The same libretto, the author of which is unknown, had had a great success with Anfossi's music in the carnival of 1774 at Rome. Perhaps this was why it was selected for Munich. At the first rehearsal, the members of the orchestra declared that they had never heard finer music, nor any in which every air was so beautiful. The first representation was on the 13th of January, 1775. Schubart speaking of it says: "I have also heard an opera-buffa by the wonderful genius, Mozart. It is called 'La Finta Giardiniera.' The flames of genius dart hither and thither; but it is not yet the still altar-fire which ascends to heaven in clouds of incense, a sweet savour unto the gods. If Mozart is not a hot-house-reared plant, he must become one of the greatest musical composers who have ever lived." It is to be observed that Mozart knew accurately the artists for whom he wrote. "La Finta Giardiniera" has maintained its superiority over the best comic operas of its day, in spite of the traditional Italian influences under which it was created. The principal performers were Rosa Manservisi and Rossi, both of whom had a great reputation. Mozart had this time the pleasure of having his sister with him to witness his triumph. Other friends from Salzburg had also come to Munich for the carnival. In the interval between the first two performances of the opera, the Archbishop Hieronymus arrived, and accepted, with many a bow and shrug of his shoulders, the congratulations he received from the Elector and the assembled court upon his concertmeister Mozart. From the archbishop's behaviour, but more particularly from the circumstance of his returning to Salzburg before the second performance, we may gather how little interest he took in the triumph of his subject.

There were great difficulties in arranging repetitions of the opera. For the lady who took the second part fell ill, added to which Tozi, the conductor of the orchestra, became involved in an intrigue with the Countess Seefeld, which ended in his sudden flight from Munich.

Mozart's sacred compositions were held in high esteem by the electoral court. On New Year's Day, 1775, his litany in B major was performed in the court chapel, and on the following Sunday two masses. A few days prior to his departure for Salzburg, the Elector expressed a wish to hear an offertory in counterpoint by Mozart, which had to be composed and studied by the next Sunday. Mozart composed the celebrated "Misericordias Domini," which Padre Martini greeted with hearty approval, but which Thibaut has found fault with in his "Reinheit der Tonkunst," p. 183, on the ground that the words of the psalmist are not treated with unity. Notwithstanding all Thibaut's objections, the "Misericordias" is one of the noblest pieces of church music ever written, both on account of its psychological qualities and its delicacy of construction. It is, moreover, to a certain extent, a type of what Mozart at nineteen was able to do in that particular branch of music.

As a pianist also he obtained great success at Munich. Schubart says of him in the "Deutsche Chronik :" "Only think, brother, what pleasure it was. Last year in Munich I heard two of the greatest performers on the pianoforte, Herr Mozart and Herr Hauptmann von Beecke. My host, Herr Albert, who is an enthusiastic admirer of the great and beautiful, has an excellent pianoforte in his house. I heard these two giants wrestle with it. Mozart plays the most difficult things that are laid before him at sight. Nothing more is needed. Beecke far surpasses him. Winged speed, grace, melting sweetness, and a self-cultivated taste peculiar to himself are weapons which no one will wrest from the hands of this Hercules." This is the first time Mozart's playing is compared with that of Beecke, who had a great reputation. Meanwhile Beecke himself was looked upon by the Archbishop Hieronymus as a charlatan and mountebank. We shall meet him again as a rival of Mozart.

Mozart hoped to be commissioned to write the serious opera for Munich for the following year. But this hope was disappointed. Probably the envious tongues of Salzburg had so often hinted that Wolfgang would settle at Munich, that the good understanding which existed between the Salzburg and Munich courts prevented the negotiation coming to anything. Father, son, and daughter remained in Munich till towards the end of the carnival, and reached Salzburg on the 7th of March, 1775. The Archduke Maximilian, youngest son of the Empress Maria Theresa, and afterwards Archbishop of Cologne, was about to visit the archiepiscopal court, and

Wolfgang received instructions immediately to set to work on the music for the festivities, which were to be arranged in honour of the princely guest. Metastasio's "Il Re pastore," which had been already set to music by Bono at Vienna in 1751, was given to him as libretto. Mozart must have been very quick over his work, which is written in the style of concert music. Besides, he could not trust much to Salzburg singers, and therefore kept to a more conventional form than in "La Finta Giardiniera." The conventionalities of the libretto, too, were a great restraint upon him. It is characteristic of his genius that Mozart both here in serious opera, and also in comic opera, placed the instrumental music upon a broader basis than was previously the custom. This feature constitutes a new departure in the creations of the young master dating from this time. As early as the 23rd of April, the opera was put upon the stage. The Salzburg singers were assisted by the soprano Consoli from Munich, on whose account the words of the principal aria were altered, and a new bravura air was composed by Mozart. On the 27th of April a "musique" in honour of the archduke was given, at the conclusion of which "the celebrated young Mozart performed on the harpsichord, and played various things out of his head with as much art as charm." Such is the account of one of the cavaliers of the archduke.

That Mozart was most industrious at this time is proved by the fact that, on the 11th of June, he composed his first violin concerto, probably after his renewed study of that instrument, with a view to obtaining more easily some appointment. The first violin concerto was followed in this same year 1775 by four others, and a large number of various works—divertimenti, sonatas, masses, &c. Notwithstanding this extended field of activity, which both directly and indirectly was to his advantage at the archiepiscopal court, the relations between the Mozarts, both father and son, and the archbishop in no way improved. To understand this rightly it will be necessary to glance at the conditions of the musical world at Salzburg, where Wolfgang dwelt uninterruptedly from the date of his return from Munich on the 7th of March, 1775, till his grand tour to Munich, Mannheim, and Paris, begun on the 23rd of Sep-

tember, 1777. As has been mentioned before, Leopold Mozart
was appointed vice-capellmeister on the 28th of February,
1763. In this post he had succeeded Guiseppe Lolli of
Bologna, who was advanced to that of capellmeister, hitherto
held by Eberlin. The post of director of the orchestra,
which Leopold had previously occupied, was bestowed on
Johann Michael Haydn (b. 1737, d. 1806), the younger
brother of Josef Haydn, who, since 1757, had been capellmeister at Grosswardein. The new leader of the orchestra
had done much for church music. Wolfgang made him his
model in this respect. He has even copied in score many
of Michael Haydn's pieces. Unfortunately Michael Haydn
loved to sit over his wine and beer, which habit occasionally
caused him to neglect the duties of his office. His wife, too,
was sometimes a "rock of offence." These things considered,
Leopold Mozart had no desire for a nearer acquaintance with
the Haydn family. Anton Cajetan Adlgasser, who had studied
in Italy, was organist. With him were associated Frane
Ignatius Lipp, father-in-law to Haydn, and since 1775 Anton
Paris. With all these, and most others of their colleagues,
both Mozarts were on friendly terms. Yet each was well
aware that the Mozart family held back, and prided itself on
its good conduct and education, and where these were wanting
in others, did not hesitate to express its contempt in jest and
sarcasm. Moreover, German musicians collectively had to
suffer from the intrigues of the Italians, who had found
their way to the court at Salzburg as to every other German
court. Such a man as Archbishop Hieronymus despised all
native talent.

Burney says it was a subject of reproach to the Salzburg Chapel that its execution was rather harsh and noisy,
than delicate and in the best taste, and that therefore
the archbishop had sent for Italians to improve its style.
Lolli was hardly fit for work any longer, so on the 5th of
September, 1772, Domenico Fischietti was appointed titular
capellmeister. Fischietti came from Dresden, having been
dismissed thence because he was not sufficiently active.
He had been employed at Dresden since 1765 as composer
and *maestro di musica* of the Bastelli opera company.
Through the recommendation of the Countess Palfy, sister
to the archbishop, he came to Salzburg, promising to do great

things. But he did so little that both the Mozarts looked upon him with some contempt, more especially as Leopold had an old established right to the post which had been given to the Italian. The soloists of the chapel were also replaced by Italians – Brunetti (violin), Ferrari (violoncello), Ferlendi (oboe), and later, the castrato Ceccarelli for singing. Michael Haydn, who, in common with the other Germans, looked with anything but satisfaction upon this Italian invasion, called them "the foreign asses." Confident of the archbishop's favour, they indulged in much that was unseemly. To the Mozarts, both father and son—the latter had been concertmeister since 1770, though without a salary—their engagement was most mortifying. We hear little of Fischietti's, but all the more of Wolfgang's compositions. It is not to be wondered at that Mozart, from his youth, looked upon Italians with suspicion. But that in spite of this prejudice, he knew how to make individual distinctions is proved by his uninterrupted and affectionate correspondence with Padre Martini of Bologna. As concertmeister, Wolfgang drew monthly no more than twelve and a half gulden (1*l.* 1*s.* 6*d.*), although new compositions were required of him on every occasion.

For the mere satisfaction of showing his contempt for Wolfgang, the archbishop would not increase the scanty pay. The unfortunate relations between Mozart and the archbishop became more embittered as often as his Grace heard that the young man's merit was acknowledged abroad, and that therefore his family thought of sending him again upon his travels. We know that to a family blest with so little worldly wealth as the Mozarts, it could be no light matter to make arrangements for a new tour. Still the necessity for it became daily more obvious if Mozart was not to fall into oblivion as a composer and virtuoso. How carefully the new tour was thought over and planned, we may gather from the fact that Wolfgang wrote out neatly a great number of his best compositions into small note-books which could be easily packed, and which would be useful either for purposes of performance or copying.

Leopold Mozart had presented a petition to the archbishop on the 14th of March, 1777, in which he prayed for an increase of salary on account of the poor circumstances of the family. No answer was vouchsafed to his request. In the early summer of 1777, the Emperor was expected to pass through Salzburg, and the archbishop had given notice that the court music was to be in readiness for the event. This was why Leopold Mozart did not apply for leave of absence as early as June. Later he made the request which the archbishop refused, with the remark that young Mozart " who, besides, is only half in service," could at any rate travel alone. To this observation, Wolfgang referred when stung by the archbishop's assertions—his Grace had said that Wolfgang knew nothing of his art, and ought to go to the Conservatoire at Naples to study—he applied for the leave of absence already refused to his father. Wolfgang wrote to the archbishop the following memorable words : " Parents take pains to put their children in a position to earn their own bread, and the children are under an obligation to themselves and to the need of the state. The greater the talents they have received from God, the greater their obligation to make use of them for the improvement of their own and their parents' circumstances, to assist their parents, and to provide for their own advancement and for the future  The Gospel teaches us this usury of talents. I am, therefore, bound before God in my conscience, with all my power to be grateful to my father, who has unweariedly devoted all his time to my education, to lighten for him the burden, and now for myself, and afterwards for my sister, to provide, for I should be sorry that she should have spent so many hours at the harpsichord without making a profitable use of them. With your Grace's leave, therefore, I most humbly pray your Grace to dismiss me from your service, for I am anxious to take advantage of the approaching autumn months, so as not to be exposed to the bad weather of the cold months which will soon follow. Your Grace will not take unfavourably this most humble prayer, since three years ago your Grace, when I begged permission to travel to Vienna, was graciously pleased to declare that I had nothing to hope for, and should do better to seek my fortune elsewhere. I thank your Grace in deepest humility for all great favours received, and with the flattering hope of being able to serve your Grace in my manhood with more approval, I commend myself to your Grace's continued favour and goodness."

The writer of these words, then one-and twenty, might well have taken for his motto: "Fortiter in re, suaviter in modo." On the 28th of August, 1777, the archbishop decreed that the father and son had permission, "according to the gospel," to seek their fortune abroad. Afterwards the archbishop declared he had refused the petition for leave of absence, because he could not suffer them "to travel about begging." In this manner father and son were dismissed. However, the archbishop denied that he had granted his dismissal to Leopold as well as to his son. The affair caused a great stir in Salzburg; even the Italian Brunetti, of whom we have spoken above, was of opinion that the archbishop had dismissed the younger Mozart to his own detriment. When the grand steward of the court, Count von Firmian, at all times a patron of the Mozart family, and particularly attached to Wolfgang, waited upon the archbishop, the latter said to him, "Now we have one person less for the music?" The count answered, "Your Grace has lost a great virtuoso." "How so?" asked the archbishop. "He is the greatest performer on the harpsichord I have ever heard in my life, he has done good service with the violin, and he is a right good composer." Whereupon his Grace was silent. The Canon Count Starhemberg also expressed himself in Mozart's favour.

The archbishop must have known best himself how discontented he had reason to be at the turn the affair had taken. Wolfgang's behaviour throughout had been manly, but the greatest admiration is due to his father, who, in order to save his family from anxiety for their daily bread, remained under these painful circumstances in his scantily paid post of vice-capellmeister. The old man—he was nearly sixty—had to resolve upon giving lessons again so as to cover, at least in part, the cost of the journey. But his greatest trouble was that he would have to let his son travel alone. To obviate this he came to the painful determination to send his mother with Wolfgang. He knew that she did not possess the requisite energy and presence of mind to guide a young man like Wolfgang continually in the right way. Still he felt sure that with his mother by his side his health at least would be cared for. The correspondence between the father and son, which often bears on this important point, is of the greatest interest, and gives us a close insight into their relations with each other. The chief necessaries for a journey being provided—a chaise even was procured that Wolfgang might make a creditable appearance —he and his mother started early on the morning of the 23rd of September, 1777. Leopold Mozart writes to them a few days afterwards:—

" After you left, I went very miserably upstairs, and threw myself down on a chair. I had been at great pains to restrain myself at our parting, so as not to make our farewell more painful, and in this agitation I forgot to give my son his father's blessing. I ran to the window, and I gave my blessing to you both, but did not see you drive out of the gate, and so must suppose you had already passed, for I had sat there a long time without thinking of anything."

Marianne cried all day, and only became calmer towards evening.

In the meantime Wolfgang and his mother were travelling into the wide world ; for him the separation had nothing painful in it, for it freed him from what he felt to be a degrading position. When he wrote to his father from Wasserburg on the evening of the day of departure, he was cheerful and full of spirits. Their first destination was Munich, where Wolfgang possessed good friends. The Intendant of Plays, Count Seeon, was aware of Mozart's dismissal from Salzburg, and being desirous that he should settle in Munich, advised him straightway to obtain an audience of the Elector. Another of Wolfgang's patrons, the Prince-bishop of Chiemsee, Count Zeil, paved the way at court for the interview. The Elector, indeed, observed that Mozart would do better to travel to Italy first, and make himself known there. At his private audience Wolfgang mentioned his performance at Bologna, when he completed in half an hour work for which musicians of standing required four or five hours. The Elector was most friendly and gracious, but, nevertheless, said there was no vacancy for an appointment at Munich. It was a very important moment for Wolfgang ; in fact, there was little to hope from the Munich Court. Count Seeon, no doubt, wished Wolfgang to settle in Munich, but in his own interests, for he was *impresario* of the theatre, and he was well aware what a treasure he would possess in the young musician. He asked the Bishop of Chiemsee if he thought that, with some assistance on his part, it would be possible for Mozart to remain in Munich. But when the bishop replied that, according to all accounts, family circumstances would hardly permit that, the count did not venture to question Mozart personally. In the meantime Mozart was delighted with German opera. The singer, Keiser, pleased him especially, notwithstanding that she appeared on the stage only for the third time. " A serious German opera they would also like to perform, and they wish me to compose it," he writes to his father. Several men of learning and position, besides musicians and amateurs (among them an ecclesiastic named Dubreil, a former pupil of Tartini), interested themselves greatly in Mozart. Everywhere he had to play, and distinguished himself as a performer both on the pianoforte and the violin. But his most enthusiastic admirer was his landlord, Herr Albert. He promised to bring together ten good friends, who should guarantee him a salary of nearly six hundred gulden if he would remain in Munich. The old father at home shook his head incredulously when he heard the news, and how completely he was in the right the result, or rather non-result, proved. For Herr Albert had no more success in finding ten such enthusiastic admirers of Mozart in Munich, than Lot in his search for ten righteous men in Sodom. Wolfgang was advised to make an agreement with Count Seeon for a yearly supply of four operas, for which he hoped to receive a fixed salary of three hundred gulden. It is evident that Wolfgang had confidence in himself in that respect, also that he believed himself capable of living on so small a salary. However, nothing came of this plan. His father was against it, and it appears Count Seeon, too.

Leopold Mozart urged a speedy departure from Munich. So Wolfgang had a farewell audience of the intendant, which he thus describes :—" Early to-day, about eight o'clock (a little early, it is true), I was with Count Seeon. I made it very short, and simply said, ' I am only here, your Excellency, to explain myself and my affairs. The reproach has been made to me that I ought to go to Italy. I was sixteen months in Italy, and wrote three operas. This is well enough known. What more I have done, your Excellency will see from these papers.' I showed him the diplomas, with the words, ' I show and tell your Excellency all this only that if I am spoken of, and, perhaps, injustice is done to me, your Excellency may with reason take my part.' He asked me if I were now going to France. I said I should still remain in Germany. But he understood in Munich, and said, with a pleased laugh, 'So, you remain here still?' I said, 'No, I would willingly remain, and, to tell the truth, I would gladly have had something from the Elector, only that I might afterwards serve your Excellency with my compositions, indeed, disinterestedly. It would be to me a pleasure.' At this he pushed his night-cap quite back." Leopold Mozart replied, "That you could live alone in Munich is possible; but what sort of honour would that be to you? how the archbishop would joke about it. You can do that in any place, not only in Munich. It does not do to make oneself so small, nor to throw oneself away. There is certainly no need for that yet." At midday, on the 11th of October, Wolfgang left Munich with his mother, and the same evening reached Augsburg, the birthplace of his father. Acting upon Leopold's advice, they took up their quarters at the "Lamb," in the Kreuzgasse, " where for dinner one pays thirty kreuzers a head, and where there are fine rooms; also persons of the greatest consequence—English, French, etc., put up there." The travellers met with a friendly reception from Leopold Mozart's brother, Joseph Ignaz, with whose daughter Maria Anna—born 14th of January, 1758, and consequently two years younger than himself—Wolfgang quickly struck up a friendship which lasted long after he had left Augsburg, and was renewed when he returned alone after his mother's death. At Augsburg Mozart's first formal visit was to the Stadtpfleger (magistrate) von Langenmantel, whose manners by no means pleased him, for he left his cousin, who had accompanied him, to wait in the hall, as if he were a servant. This absurd affectation of superiority on the part of the Stadtpfleger reminded Leopold of Wieland's Abderite. His next visit, to the celebrated organ and harpsichord builder, Georg Andreas Stein (1728-92), made a much better impression on Wolfgang. Unfortunately he was obliged to accept the escort of the Stadtpfleger's son, who introduced Wolfgang instantly with the words, " I have the honour to present to you a virtuoso on the harpsichord."

As, according to his father's advice, Mozart was to appear

incognito at Stein's, he hastily interrupted him by saying that he was only an unworthy pupil of Herr Sigl at Munich, from whom he was the bearer of a thousand compliments. Stein shook his head incredulously, and observed, " Have I the honour to see Herr Mozart before me ? "   " Oh, no," said Wolfgang, whose father had written to him to introduce himself to Stein under a feigned name, and to pretend that he came from Innsbruck to look at instruments; he thereupon gave the anagram of his name " Trazom." However, a letter which Mozart delivered to Stein from his father soon put an end to the joke. Stein was overjoyed to see the young artist at his house. In a long letter to his father, Mozart sets forth the advantages of Stein's harpsichords. We read therein, to the great credit of this able man, that "he works only with a view to the requirements of the musician, and not merely according to his own necessities." Stein was a passionate lover of music. On this occasion Mozart mentions for the first time the pedal, which he calls "the machine on which one presses with the knee." This also is better in Stein's harpsichords than in others. He scarcely needs to touch it; it moves directly, and "as soon as one moves one's knee away a little, not the least after-sound is audible." Mozart's playing so won the favour of the harpsichord-maker that he asked his advice concerning the education of his daughter, Anna Maria, born in 1769, who was looked upon as the wonder of Augsburg. In April, 1776, she had given her first concert, and had received a handsome medal from the great folks of the place. Mozart criticized her playing somewhat severely ; still he said, " She may improve ; she has genius, but she will never master the chief point in music, that is the 'tempo,' because from childhood upwards she has not studied to perfection the art of playing in time."

This and similar observations of Mozart on harpsichord playing, enable us to form a clear conception of what he required both of himself and others on this point. Mention has been made above of Beecke, with whom Mozart underwent comparison at Munich in the year 1775. For this man Stein, as Wolfgang writes to his father, had quite an infatuation. " Now that he sees and hears that I play better than Beecke, that I make no grimaces, and yet play with expression, he acknowledges no one has ever used his instruments so well. The accurate time I keep is the admiration of everybody. The 'tempo rubato' in an adagio—that my left hand is not concerned in it, for with them the left hand gives way. Count Wolfegg, and several others who are warm champions of Beecke, said the other day publicly at the concert, that I put Beecke in the shade. Count Wolfegg kept running about the room saying, ' I have heard nothing like it in my life.' To me he said, ' I must say that I have never heard you play as you played to-day. I shall tell your father so, too, as soon as I get back to Salzburg.' "

The concert of which Wolfgang is speaking took place on the 22nd of October, and on this occasion his concerto for three pianos was performed in public for the first time. Demler the organist played one instrument, Mozart the second, and Stein the third. An "incomparable article," probably emanating from Zabnesing, appeared on the concert, in the "Maschenbauerische Zeitung," No. 213, which gave great satisfaction to Leopold Mozart. The pecuniary results were certainly not brilliant ; the concert only brought in about seventy gulden clear profit. For his services in the "vornehme Bauernstub-Akademie," under the patronage of both Catholics and Lutherans of distinction, Mozart received but two ducats ; encomiums, however, were much more liberally bestowed on him. He was quite justified in writing to his father : "This I can say, if it were not for such a good cousin and such a dear Bäsle (little cousin), I should have as many regrets as I have hairs on my head, that I am at Augsburg." Marie Anne, the " Bäsle," greatly resembled Mozart in temperament. . " We two go well together," he writes to his father. Both were naturally merry, and fond of fun and jokes, at which they themselves laughed most. Mozart retained in after-years his love of humour ; it acted as a counterpoise to the mental strain he underwent when alone. His merry intercourse with his cousin strikingly contrasts with the earnest converse he held with Stein upon music and the building of harpsichords, and is a witness to the fresh, healthy mode of thought which afterwards penetrated his dramatic works to such a remarkable degree. Mozart presented his cousin with a small medallion portrait of himself, and begged his father to allow him to give her as a keepsake, some one of the many presents which remained to him from his early travels. When the hour of separation came there was a sorrowful parting. At Salzburg people laughed pleasantly at the natural and charming affection of the two young folks. The chief delight of the Salzburg family and their friends was shooting with the bow. At the first opportunity they had the two young people, Wolfgang and the Bäsle, dissolved in tears, painted on the target. Leopold Mozart gives us an exact description of it. An Augsburg maiden stood on the right, and was presenting a young man, booted and otherwise ready for a journey, with a parting nosegay. In her other hand she held a linen cloth, trailing on the floor, with which she dried her eyes. The " chapeau " had a similar cloth, was also drying his eyes, and held his hat in his other hand. Beneath were inscribed some verses alluding to. the happy time the cousins had spent together.

Leopold Mozart was, as we see, always ready to sympathize with his son's pleasures ; still he knew that, following his advice, Wolfgang had already set out on his quest for fresh honour and renown. To the good wishes addressed to him on his saint's-day, Wolfgang answered, " Papa may be easy ; I have God always before my eyes. I acknowledge His omnipotence, I fear His wrath, but I also acknowledge His love, His pity, and His mercy towards His creatures ; He will never forsake His servants. Whatever is according to His will is also according to mine ; therefore I cannot fail to be happy and contented." Worthy of all admiration and envy is the harmony of soul which could conceive thoughts so sublime, and yet was capable of appreciating and enjoying the things of this earth to their full extent. Only the soul of a great artist could possess such delicate susceptibilities.

On the 26th of October Mozart travelled with his mother through Donauwörth and Nördlingen to Hohenaltheim, the residence of Prince Oetting-Wallerstein, a passionate lover of music. The prince's intendant of court music was Mozart's rival, Captain Beecke, frequently mentioned in these pages. Unfortunately the prince, who had known Wolfgang before in Naples, was in such a melancholy frame of mind that he could listen to no music. Still as Frau Mozart was suffering from a cold, the travellers remained at the castle for a few days. Beecke was most civil to Wolfgang, and gave him advice in case of his visiting Paris. In further conversation Beecke and Wolfgang mutually agreed that music soon gave them a headache. Wolfgang was affected in this way by bad, Beecke even by good music.

On the 30th of October, Mozart reached Mannheim, a town destined to play an important part, in the development of his musical talent, and of his character. The day after his arrival he was introduced to the Director of Music, Cannabich, who took him to the rehearsal of a Magnificat by Vogel. Some of the musicians present were very polite, others stared at him so rudely that he wrote to his father: "They think because I am little and young that there can be nothing great and old in me ; but they will soon see."

Mozart was well advised in making it a point of honour to acquire a reputation at Mannheim. In those days Mannheim ranked first as a musical city. Poets like Wieland and Klopstock travelled thither for the sake of its music. Even abroad the Mannheim method of teaching music was followed. Lord Fordyce declared, as Schubart relates, that Prussian tactics and Mannheim music placed the Germans above all other nations. Wieland's commendable idea of creating a grand German opera, which found expression in "Alceste," set to music by Schweitzer, was encouraged by the Mannheim Elector, Karl Theodor, who was desirous of having that work performed in the theatre of his castle at Schwetzingen. Thus it came to pass, and a remarkable event it was, that on the 13th of August, 1775, a German opera, written by a German, composed by a German, and sung by German singers before a German prince, was put upon the stage with great success. Wieland received a commission to write a new opera, for which Schweitzer was again to compose the music. The Elector intended also to represent the legends of the fatherland upon the boards of his opera-house at Mannheim. With this end in view the "philosopher," Anton Klein, of Mannheim, wrote the opera "Günther von Schwarzburg," the music being com-

F

posed by Capellmeister Holzbauer. Mozart heard this work the day after his arrival, and bestowed high praise upon the music, while censuring the libretto. He was surprised that so old a man as Holzbauer, who was then sixty-six, should still retain so much genius. The work was not without its influence on the "aria concertante" of Mozart. It was Holzbauer's merit to have made the orchestra an important feature in the Italian aria from the influence of which he was never able to free himself entirely. Under Holzbauer's tuition, the German singers, Dorothea Wendling, "the German Melpomene of the golden age of Mannheim," her sister-in-law, Elizabeth Augusta Wendling, and Franciska Danzi, had made considerable progress, so that, when assisted by an artist of the first rank like Anton Raaff, they formed an excellent ensemble.

Raaff, born in 1714, at Holzem, near Bonn, was indebted to the liberality of Clement Augustus, Elector of Cologne, for his musical education. In course of time, he studied with Bernachi at Bologna, assisted as a singer at the marriage of Maria Theresa at Florence, and had a series of triumphs at Vienna, Lisbon, Madrid, and Naples. In 1770 the Elector Karl Theodor summoned him to enter his service. Unfortunately his voice, once the wonder of the world, was greatly on the decline when Mozart heard him at Mannheim for the first time, and in his next letter to Salzburg Wolfgang makes fun of him. However, they soon became excellent friends. Leopold Mozart had written to his son that Raaff was the person of all others in Mannheim whom he might completely trust. Raaff was an honest, God-fearing man, who liked Germans, so Leopold said, and his description of the veteran artist—at that time he was sixty-three—was an accurate one.

Besides the singers already mentioned, there were in the chapel of the Elector a number of meritorious artists, foremost amongst whom stood Christian Cannabich, capellmeister since 1775. He was an able violinist, and almost without exception the younger members of the orchestra had been his pupils. Moreover, he possessed remarkable individuality of character, which, together with his blameless life, had the best possible influence upon his pupils, by whom he was held in great esteem. Under his guidance the orchestra of Mannheim distinguished itself, its execution especially being noted for delicacy of light and shade, so that it was held to be the first in Europe. It was here that Mozart for the first time heard clarinets in the orchestra. "Ah, if we only had clarinets!" he sighed, thinking of Salzburg. The praises bestowed by contemporaries upon the orchestra of Mannheim culminate in Schubart's words: "No orchestra in the world has ever excelled that of Mannheim in execution. Its *forte* is thunder, its *crescendo* a cataract, its *diminuendo* like the far-off rippling of a crystal stream, its *piano* the breath of spring." Although such a description may appear somewhat exaggerated, yet an association of artists as distinguished as those who worked together at Mannheim enables us to draw our own conclusions as to the excellence of their performance in a body, more particularly as Stamitz, the predecessor in office of Cannabich, had established the discipline of the orchestra in a most exemplary manner, and Cannabich had followed his traditions with the utmost zeal.

Naturally Mozart was soon on intimate terms with the musicians. The friendship of Cannabich, which he had gained rapidly, led to a cordial intimacy with the capellmeister's family. In this intimacy Mozart's mother shared. The family always kept up the truest friendship for their Salzburg visitors, and tried to be useful to them wherever it was possible. Cannabich's eldest daughter Rosa inspired Mozart with singular interest; "a beautiful and charming girl; for her age she has a great deal of sense and stability of character; she is serious, and does not say much, but what she does say is said with grace and courtesy." Mozart found that she played the pianoforte agreeably. He began immediately to compose a sonata for her, the andante of which, as he himself said, "he intended to make just like the character of Mdlle. Rosa." It is probably the sonata in B major (Köchel, 281). He also studied the sonata with the young lady, and instructed her generally in a regular manner, giving her a lesson daily. Another Mannheim beauty, the daughter of the flute-player Joh. Bapt. Wendling, the husband of the singer mentioned above, inspired him to the composition of two French songs. Augusta Wendling must have been very beautiful, for Wieland considered her so like one of Raphael's Madonnas that a person looking at her would scarcely be able to turn away his eyes. For her mother Mozart sketched an aria after Metastasio, and for her father he executed the instrumentation of one of the concertos for the flute written by that musician. Very soon a plan was formed to make a journey to Paris in company with Wendling, in which Ramm, the excellent oboist was also to take part. Ramm that same winter performed Mozart's oboe-concerto, originally composed for Ferlendi at Salzburg, no less than five times.

With two exceptions Mozart appears to have been on friendly terms with all the musicians of Mannheim. The exceptions were the celebrated Abbé Vogler and his follower Joh. Peter Winter, almost the only intimate friend and companion Vogler had. At his first meeting with Vogler, when the latter played upon the pianoforte, Mozart took a decided dislike to him, perhaps because he had already been prejudiced against him, for Vogler was regarded by all the musicians as an intruder and *intriguant*. Mozart vehemently abused Vogler's playing to his father. Vogler was a man of mark and great intellect. Gifted with remarkable strength of will, he had acquired an absolute command over the technical elements of music. His creative power, however, is of minor importance. He is the father of the modern musical "effect" so decisively and justly condemned by Richard Wagner, which, indeed, Weber, one of Vogler's celebrated pupils, knew how to guard against, but which the other, Meyerbeer, used in such a glaring manner. That Mozart should hold in but little esteem a man so bent upon external things, however he might impose on others, is intelligible. Mozart courageously uttered his opinion of Vogler to every one. Still there is no proof that Vogler, as Leopold Mozart supposed, used his influence in opposition to Mozart at Mannheim. The efforts of the latter were directed towards obtaining employment from the Elector, either in the writing of an opera, or in the regular instruction of the children of the Elector; in short, a definite appointment. The Elector's children were indeed confided to his care, but his desire for an appointment was cautiously ignored. When Mozart pressed the Elector for a decisive answer, he was at last informed, on the 8th of December, 1777, through the intendant, Count Savioli, that the Elector had no intention of giving Mozart a place. The decision, so unexpected, was most painful to Mozart's friends. The family of Cannabich, in particular, showed their sympathy. Tears even were shed when the news came of Mozart's departure, now impending.

Wendling, who was desirous not to lose his illustrious travelling companion to Paris, set everything in motion to prolong Mozart's stay at Mannheim. He had induced a rich Dutchman, named Déjean or Déchamp, to give Mozart two hundred gulden for a few short compositions. Cannabich was to procure lessons for him. Mozart was to dine and sup with Wendling, and be lodged free of expense by the court councillor Serrarius. Besides this his sonata for pianoforte and violin was to be published by subscription. It is true he was to separate from his mother, for whom a lodging was to be found in an obscure and cheap quarter of the town. This separation did not meet with the father's approval. Being winter, the mother could not think of returning home, as she had declared herself ready to do in the event of Wolfgang's travelling to Paris with Wendling. Moreover, Leopold Mozart wished, for obvious reasons, that mother and son should be together, so long as the latter remained at Mannheim. He hinted in a letter to his son that Wolfgang's gaiety of disposition might lead him into bad ways, to which Wolfgang, somewhat hurt, replied: "I am gay, but be assured that I can be in earnest as well as any one." In the dilemma Serrarius came to the rescue. He took both mother and son into his house, in return for which Wolfgang was to instruct his talented daughter Theresa Pierron, then fifteen years old. To her Mozart dedicated one of his most beautiful sonatas for pianoforte and violin (Köchel, 296). In this way a convenient solution was found for the chief difficulty. Mozart also obtained, as a pupil, a Dutch officer, De la Potrie. In the letters exchanged with Salzburg about this time, a happy, cheerful tone is once more discernible. Not without feelings of pride must Leopold Mozart have learnt what high estimation and love was on all sides given to his son, who had now grown to be a young man, and whose beard could no longer be cut with the scissors, but had to be entrusted to the barber.

At the end of December Wieland came to Mannheim to

be present at the last rehearsals of his opera "Rosamunde," composed by Schweitzer. Naturally Mozart was eager to make the acquaintance of the celebrated poet. However, he was not much edified by his personal appearance. He expresses himself plainly enough on this point. "He seems to me a little affected in conversation, has rather a childish voice, a continual stare, a certain learned roughness, and yet at times a silly condescension. But I am not surprised that he is pleased so to conduct himself here, for people look upon him as if he had come down from heaven." Later on he says that Wieland, after hearing him play, and paying him every possible compliment, said, "It is a real pleasure to me to have met you here." After all "Rosamunde" was not performed, for on the 30th of December, the Elector Maximilian of Bavaria died, and the Elector Karl Theodor, his successor, travelled with all haste to Munich, where he took up his residence. In the meantime the prospect of an appointment for Mozart at Vienna appeared on the horizon, for the Emperor Joseph wished to found a national German comic opera in that city. Mozart heard of it, and begged his father to make inquiries about the matter through his friends at Vienna. The answer sent by one of these friends was not very encouraging. "Gluck and Salieri are already in the Emperor's service; a young artist like Wolfgang could only assert himself by sending to Vienna a German opera composed at a venture."[2] Wolfgang felt hurt at this demand.

When February came, and the journey to Paris had to be seriously thought of, Wolfgang suddenly informed his father that he wished to give up the idea. All at once he re-

---

[2] At the same time that this letter left Vienna for Salzburg, Wolfgang was travelling—it was towards the end of January—to Kircheim-Boland to visit the Princess of Orange, at the recommendation of the Dutch officer previously mentioned. He was accompanied by the copyist and prompter of the Mannheim National Theatre, Fridolin von Weber, a man in very moderate circumstances, and his daughter Aloysia, a girl of fifteen, and a clever singer. They were well received; nevertheless, Wolfgang had to content himself with the magnificent reward of seven louis-d'ors for playing twelve times and for the dedication of four symphonies. Aloysia Weber had five louis-d'ors. On the return journey they stayed five days at Worms, where the travellers amused themselves in various ways, and endeavoured to forget the annoyance caused by the wretched pay.

marked that Wendling was without any religion; Ramm was known to him as a libertine, and the idea of travelling in company with men whose mode of thinking differed from his own suddenly alarmed Wolfgang, and made him draw back. Naturally his father was astonished that these complaints were heard for the first time now, after mother and son had been long acquainted with their intended travelling-companions. Still, although he earnestly tried to induce his son to overcome his sudden aversion to Wendling, and to go to Paris with him, he did not do so without some pangs of anxiety. On the 15th of February, 1778, the two travellers set out alone. Wolfgang comforted his father by saying, "The way to Paris is always open to me." It was somewhat surprising to the old gentleman that Wolfgang had written shortly before this: "I get along quite easily here; besides, there is the music for Déjean; for that I shall obtain my two hundred florins. I can remain here as long as I like; neither board nor lodging costs me anything." Leopold Mozart bitterly reproached his son with not having executed the commission to supply the Dutchman with compositions, notwithstanding that he was contemplating a journey to Paris, and that he had made an excursion to Kirchheim-Boland with Weber. "How would it be," observed the anxious old man, tormented by grief and care for his family, "if M. Déjean should not keep his word?" Unfortunately, through Wolfgang's negligence, the affair came to an unsatisfactory conclusion. Wolfgang was obliged to say that he could not supply the whole of the order, and the Dutchman did not pay even half of the price agreed on.

It was a heavy blow for Leopold Mozart. He had reckoned on this apparently sure source of income; now he saw that he would be obliged to borrow money to provide further means for his son's journey. It soon became clear to him what sort of cause it was that made Wolfgang wish to prolong his stay at Mannheim. He was passionately in love with Aloysia Weber. Under his guidance the young girl had discovered her brilliant gifts. It was quite natural that Mozart should fall in love with this young beauty, whom, with prophetic insight, he saw surrounded by the halo of a great artist, and that Aloysia should return his passion. Mozart studied with her all his arias. At an "academy"

arranged by Cannabich, he had the delight of seeing both
his pupils, Rosa Cannabich and Aloysia, distinguished by
storms of applause.   Even Raaff could not forbear to praise
Mdlle Weber.   To words by Metastasio, already set to music
by the London Bach (whose composition pleased Mozart so
extraordinarily that it always ran in his head), he wrote a
new melody for Aloysia from the depths of his loving heart.
At the next " academy " of Cannabich his pupil, the goddess
of his heart, sang this air, for which every one was full of
praise.   At the same concert the three ladies, Rosa Cannabich, Aloysia Weber, and Theresa Pierron, played the con
certo for three pianofortes.   The new aria " Non so donde
viene " soon acquired great celebrity.   It gives us an idea
of Aloysia's powerful voice, as also of her sklll and artistic
execution.

It is quite intelligible that under such circumstances Mozart
should feel no inclination to set out for Paris.   He seriously
cherished the idea of marrying Aloysia, and his only wish
besides was to write an opera in which she might appear.   He
advised the Weber family to go to Italy, where he hoped he
might himself obtain commissions for operas.   He would
even supply the score for about thirty *zechine* (Venetian
ducats), if only she might through it become famous.   He
implored his father to enter into this project, and to apply to
the old friend of the family at Verona, Lugiati, on this
behalf.   Leopold Mozart was deeply perplexed at the new
turn affairs had taken.   After he had recovered from the
first shock, he bitterly, and yet affectionately reproached his
son with having lost sight hitherto of the real aim of his
journey :   that of making himself a man famous in the
world, and of earning sufficient money to supply for a time
the most necessary wants of life.   He sketched the whole
journey with bitter irony, continually pointing out how Wolfgang confided too much to the first-comer who praised and
extolled him ; how each new confidant invariably supplanted
the last ; how he had gone from Cannabich to Wendling,
from Wendling to Weber.   Each had always been the best
and most honest of friends till he had found a better.   " Now
this family (Weber's) is the most honest, the most Christian
family, and the daughter is the chief person in the tragedy
which is acting between your own and this family, and in all

that in the tumult into which your heart, so open and kind for everybody, has led you, you, without sufficient reflection, picture to yourself with so much exactness and infallibility, as if things must quite naturally so fall out"—so runs the father's anxious and terribly-involved sentence. He then endeavours to make clear to his son the difficulties he would have to encounter in attempting to make a prima donna out of a young girl without stage experience, how Gluck even had had trouble with Bernasconi. He places before him the absurdity of his desire that old Weber should travel to Italy with his family, and that he (Wolfgang) should accompany them. Leopold Mozart's clear understanding perceived that energetic measures must be used here. So he exclaims to his son: "Off with you to Paris, and that soon ; get the great folks on your side, 'aut Cæsar aut nihil.' The mere notion of seeing Paris should have preserved you from all fleeting fancies. From Paris the name and fame of a man of great talent goes through the whole world." Then he complains of the want of confidence and sincerity displayed by his wife and son, in not openly and circumstantially reporting to him all that passed, and winds up with an appeal to his son's good heart to look on him more as a candid friend than a severe father. Moreover Leopold Mozart does not omit to express his sympathy for the straitened circumstances of the Weber family. Wolfgang, he says, might induce Raaff, who was acquainted with Italian *impresari*, to recommend Aloysia after she had made her *début* at Mannheim.

The result of this categorical admonition was that Wolfgang saw his error. Much of it touched him to the quick, especially the thought that his father's confidence in him was shaken. So he opens his overburdened heart to his father. "I am," he says, "a Mozart, but a young, well-disposed Mozart." Mother and son now prepared for the departure from Mannheim. Leopold Mozart when he hears of it gives the most affectionate advice. From the letters which now follow, we realize, for the first time, how fondly the old man clings to his family. As might have been expected, all who knew Wolfgang saw his departure with reluctance. An affecting farewell was taken of the Weber family. The father was happy to see his son for the present rescued from the dangers of an unfortunate connexion. Without reserve Wolfgang spoke of his further correspondence with the Weber family. Father and son, too, could look confidently into the future.

On the 14th of March, Mozart and his mother started. They made an arrangement with a hackney coachman, who bought their travelling-carriage from them. After nine and a half days' travelling, they entered Paris. They put up at the hotel "Les quatre Fils Aymon" in the Rue Gros Chenet, as the Rue du Sentier between the Rue de Cléry and the Rue des Jeuneurs was then called. The travellers were contented with a little dingy room, so narrow that a pianoforte could not even be got into it. Wolfgang's next care was to seek out Baron Grimm, the old friend of the family. The ballet-master Noverre, Wendling, and Ramm had smoothed the way for him, and we hear no more of the one's want of religion, or of the other's loose principles. All at once Wendling stands revealed as a great philanthropist. Raaff, too, who came to Paris later on, met with just appreciation from Wolfgang, whom he inspired with confidence because he approved of the young man's love for Aloysia. Raaff introduced him also to the Palatine Ambassador Count von Sickingen, to whom Baron von Gemmingen and Cannabich had recommended him. His Mannheim friends, moreover, made him acquainted with the director of the "Concert Spirituel," Legros. The latter immediately commissioned him to write some new choruses and recitatives for a Miserere of Holzbauer. Gossec approved the hastily-written work, and said the first chorus was charming, and would certainly make a good impression. But at the performance not even Mozart's name figured in the programme. Much also was omitted. For the Mannheim artists, Wendling, Ramm, and Ritter, with whom was the horn-player Punto, Mozart began to compose a *sinfonia concertante* which was to be performed at one of the next concerts, but this was prevented by the intrigues of Cambini. The symphony itself has disappeared, leaving no traces.

Mozart's next acquaintances were the Duke de Guines and his amiable daughter, the latter a skilled performer on the harp. From them he straightway received a commission to write a concerto for the flute and harp, the two instruments he could not endure. However the concerto proved very fine. Wealth of melody, an interesting harmonic treatment, a bright and richly varied play of instruments, and a wonderful effect of sound—these are its claims to excellence. The duke further commissioned Mozart to instruct his daughter in composition. The lady, though not without talent, wearied of the tuition, and, as she was wanting in zeal, Wolfgang also lost all pleasure in the task for which his father reproached him. Finally the duke expected him to be satisfied with three louis-d'ors, which he scornfully sent back. As a general rule, Mozart was not fortunate in his attempts to give lessons. He complains to his father that he would willingly take the trouble if only the distances in Paris were not so great, and that he must spend nearly as much in conveyances as he received in payment. Of French people in general he does not speak well. They were not so polite by a long way as fif-teen years before, when, for the first time, the Mozart family visited Paris. It is easy of explanation. At that time he was a lovable, charming boy, and every one was interested to see him and hear him play. He was now a young man, and Paris was not the right field for him. Grimm's introductions, too, were not of much use.

With great exactness Mozart describes a visit he paid by his recommendation to the Duchess de Chabot, where he was left to wait in the cold, and then asked to play upon a pianoforte which was out of tune. Moreover, he committed the great mistake of refusing a fixed appointment open to him through the mediation of Rodolphe, the famous horn-player, author of a well-known collection of solfeggi. The appointment was that of organist at Versailles, with a salary of two thousand livres. But that seemed not sufficient for Paris. Although his father was very much taken with this appointment, because it would keep Wolfgang in continual communication with the court, and might thus lead to a capellmeistership, he followed the advice of Baron Grimm, who looked upon Versailles as a town where a man could earn nothing, and where his talents would be buried. It might be supposed that the baron gave Mozart an opportunity of earning money in Paris. But he, too, had shown far more interest in the boy-prodigy than he now did in the young man. Vague hopes of the composition of an opera thereupon revealed themselves. Leopold Mozart admonished his son carefully to study the language, and whenever he composed vocal music to submit it to his friends Grimm and Noverre for their approval.

In the meantime, Noverre found it very convenient to make use of Mozart, who was always ready and willing to compose an incidental ballet, without asking a single sou for his trouble. When Mozart had written the whole of the music required by Noverre for the ballet, "Les Petits Riens," it was produced without his name being once mentioned. His friend Grimm, too, in his "Correspondance Littéraire," mentioned the ballet, but said nothing of Mozart's music. Otto Jahn, Mozart's biographer, *par excellence*, regarded the music as lost. Some years since, however, the work was discovered in the library of the Grand Opera at Paris. Notwithstanding the rapidity with which it was evidently written, connoisseurs praise the music as very graceful. Certainly Mozart did not compose all the pieces of the ballet; he himself names "altogether twelve pieces" as his work. Careful examination gives fourteen pieces. The overture written for a large orchestra, reminds us in its form of that to Gluck's "Orpheus." On the 12th of June, 1778, the first representation took place—the second on the 20th. The ballet was given in conjunction with Piccini's "Finte gemelle," which, however, was soon set aside; while the ballet of Noverre, in which the celebrated dancers Guimard, Allard, and Asselin competed with each other, kept the stage in spite of the somewhat objectionable subject. We hear no more of an opera for the "Académie royale de la Musique." Mozart was more fortunate with the symphony in D major, which he was commissioned by Legros to write for the "Concert Spirituel." He praised himself to his friends when he submitted the work to them for not having missed the "premier coup-d'archet," on account of which the Paris orchestra was famous. The symphony was performed for the first time on the 18th of June, 1778, the feast of Corpus Christi. It went so badly at rehearsal, that Mozart would not go to the concert openly, and towards evening crept into the orchestra, as he relates, to take the instrument out of the hands of the first violin, La Houssaye, and direct the piece himself in case of necessity. Luckily, this was not needed. The symphony made a great success. "I went in my joy immediately to the Palais Royal, took an excellent ice, said my rosary

—which I had promised to do—and went home," he writes to Salzburg.

His success raised him in the estimation of Legros, who wished him to insert a lighter and more intelligible andante, which he did. The symphony with the new andante was repeated on the 15th of August, with equal success. As a concession to Paris taste, no part of the symphony was repeated. Mozart, too, was of opinion that "short and good" is best. A second symphony, according to the "Journal de Paris," was performed at the concert of the 8th of September, shortly before Mozart's departure from Paris. In the last letter written by Mozart to his father from Paris, dated the 11th of September, he expressly states : "I have come to much honour through my *two* symphonies." And from Nancy he writes on his journey home, that he had sold the two symphonies to Legros. Of this second symphony, however, no trace has been found up to the present. Most likely this work is also in the archives of the Grand Opera, where the collection of music belonging to the "Concert Spirituel" found its way. Some pianoforte sonatas with violin obbligato, begun at Mannheim, were completed at Paris. The series of six sonatas, with a dedication to the Electress Palatine of Bavaria, was brought out by the publisher Sieber, who paid Mozart fifteen louis-d'ors for it. Mozart also composed at that time a capriccio for his sister's saint's-day. Mozart was apparently in the right path to appease the fate which had been against him in his love affairs, when a new misfortune befell him, though through it the young man suddenly gained independence of character. We know that Mozart's mother accompanied him to Paris. While he went out a great deal, she remained at home in the dull, close lodging, wretchedly tended. In May she fell ill. After a few weeks she appeared to get better again. Towards the middle of June, during a tropical heat, she again became ill, and from the 19th of June was obliged to keep her bed. She allowed herself to be bled by a friar, but refused to see a physician, however much her son pressed her to do so. She had no confidence in French doctors. At last Mozart found a German surgeon, who ordered her rhubarb and wine. Her condition grew worse day by day. A physician sent by Grimm could do nothing for her, and, after a long agony, she died on the evening of the 3rd of July. Wolfgang had only left his mother's sick-bed in order to fetch an old friend of the family, Heina, the trumpeter of the King's Guard of Light Horse, whom his mother had several times visited.

During the night following his mother's death, he gathered courage to write to Salzburg. He told all the particulars to his friend Bullinger, asking him to break the sad news to his father as gently as possible. To his father he himself wrote that his mother was dangerously ill. Leopold Mozart had just begun a letter to his wife with good wishes for her saint's-day, when the news came that her illness had taken a dangerous turn. As ten days had elapsed from the date of the letter, the poor man well knew that in the interval a crisis must have been passed. Bullinger came to visit the family. Leopold Mozart guessed what had happened, and as he appeared collected, his friend told him the sad truth. "You may be easy on my account," he continues in his letter, now addressed to Wolfgang only, "I shall behave like a man. Think what a tender, loving mother you had, even as you will love me more in your maturer years when I shall be dead." A few days after, the sad news arrived from Wolfgang also. His letter bears witness to the noble and beautiful affection which bound him to his family at home. At the same time, it evinces a manliness and genuine earnestness which we seek for in vain in his earlier letters. One thought alone fills his mind—that father and sister should take care of themselves, for he is conscious of the sad loss they have just sustained. "Remember," he exclaims, "that you have a son and brother who will use all his power to make you happy, well knowing that you also will some day not refuse him the wish which does him honour, and will use all means in order to see him happy." There is no sentence in the whole letter which gives us so deep an insight into Wolfgang's character as this. Openness of heart and generosity pervade it. Face to face with the sad loss which the family had sustained, and himself more especially, for he now stood alone in a foreign land, he thought of the two problems of his life, the happiness, on the one hand, of father and sister, and, on the other, of the Weber family, to whose daughter he was bound by the strong tie of love. With great detail he relates in this letter, and in later ones, everything that could interest his father. Leopold Mozart was naturally anxious as to what would become of Wolfgang in the great foreign city; for, as Wolfgang had never concerned himself with the littlenesses of life, it was to be feared he would many a time be imposed upon and deceived.

In the meantime Grimm, or rather by his recommendation, his friend, Mdme. d'Epinay, had taken care of Mozart, and had a room assigned to him in her hotel in the Rue de la Chaussée d'Antin, where he generally found a hearty welcome. This connexion with Grimm put the difference of their characters in a striking light. Grimm had protected Mozart as a boy, but now he did not find the right means to help him. He made no secret of spurring him on to greater diligence than he had hitherto displayed, the more as he had no suspicion of the importance of the genius which as yet remained partially hidden in Mozart. As Grimm himself was in favour of Italian music as opposed to the French school, he endeavoured to persuade the young musician that he should learn from the Italian Piccini, Gluck's celebrated opponent, and others. Mozart's desire to write an opera increased in consequence; for he was eager to show his patron Grimm that he could do as well as Piccini, although he was only a German. In the conversations upon music which at that time took place between Grimm and Mozart, the young musician must have held very decided views upon Italian opera, otherwise Grimm, an enthusiast for the Italian school, would not have ceased to entertain, as he did, the expectations he had formed of Mozart's future. But Mozart had perceived with great acuteness that he could scarcely learn anything more from the Italian school, though he might perhaps get new suggestions from Gluck and Grétry. A friend of Mozart relates that in Paris he always found him busy with French scores. To his question whether there were nothing to be learnt from the Italians, Mozart answered: " As far as melody is concerned, yes; but as far as dramatic effect is concerned, no. Besides the scores which you see here, except those of Grétry, are by Gluck, Piccini, Salieri, and have nothing French about them but the words." In a letter to Leopold Mozart, written in French, Grimm declared that he did not expect any very useful result from his son's stay in Paris. The remark confirmed Leopold in the desire of his heart that Wolfgang might leave Paris as soon as possible. It was at any rate a great risk to leave an

excitable and inexperienced young man quite by himself in
that capital.

Wolfgang was very anxious to be appointed capellmeister to the Elector Karl Theodor, who now lived at
Munich. In that case he would have a near prospect of
being able to improve the straitened circumstances of the
Webers, and might lead home his Aloysia as his bride. His
father tried to induce Padre Martini to use his influence both
directly, and indirectly through Raaff, with the Elector to
this end. Meanwhile war threatened to break out. The
Mannheim court-music also was transferred to Munich, and
so it came about that the Webers now lived at Munich,
where their circumstances, through increasing debt, daily
grew worse. While Mozart was expecting that Karl Theodor
would assist him, a new prospect opened of an appointment
at Salzburg. Influential friends of the Mozart family, and
especially Count Starhemberg, were desirous of having Mozart
installed as organist and successor to the deceased Adlgasser.
The archbishop even declared to those around him that
Mozart far excelled every other competitor. In the meantime the Salzburg capellmeister Lolli also died. Leopold
Mozart perceived that the moment was a favourable one
to procure for his son a fixed appointment, and thereby
to improve the family circumstances. His next care was
to get his tried friend Bullinger to write to Wolfgang,
saying that he should take into consideration his duty
as a son, and accept this fixed appointment at Salzburg. To make it more palatable to Wolfgang, Bullinger
added that the archbishop intended to engage a second
female singer, and that his choice might fall on Aloysia
Weber. At first Mozart would hear nothing of a return to
Salzburg, which was no place for talent. When his father
explained to him that their united salaries from the archbishop would amount to a thousand gulden, and added that
Wolfgang was only to leave Paris in the event of the archbishop agreeing to the demand, the young man still hoped
the affair might come to nothing through the excessive
meanness of the archbishop. On the 13th of August, however, Leopold Mozart reported that the archbishop had
agreed to everything, and had even apologized for not being
able to make Wolfgang capellmeister. His Grace would also

grant any leave of absence required for the composition and representation of an opera.

In Leopold Mozart's opinion, Salzburg, as a central point between Vienna, Munich, and Italy, was the place of all others to live in, so as to be at hand if there were any question of undertaking an opera. The archbishop, too, was very curious about Aloysia Weber. This interesting letter concludes with the words, " My next letter will tell you that you are to set out." Wolfgang could now no long er resist. The thought of seeing his father and sister again, of being in a measure reinstated in his former position, and the prospect of having the Webers and his beloved Aloysia near him at Salzburg were too tempting. He was in the best of spirits, and he begged his father's permission to make the return journey through Mannheim, so that he might visit the Webers. His father was glad to get him only so far. With a certain magnanimity he told his son he was not to suppose that he, his father, had anything against his acquaintance with Mdlle. Weber. All young people must be foolish. This was a little annoying to the tender lover. As, however, the Webers had, in the meantime, acquired a better position, and as Mozart himself had not given up all hope of being likewise appointed to the Electoral Court in Munich, he was very desirous that his father should realize the durability of his relations with Aloysia. It was his intention to make every effort in Mannheim and Munich to be taken into the service of the Elector, and thus to "make a fool" of the archbishop. His father, perceiving that for the present his efforts would be in vain, let him have his way ; he even gave him instructions how to proceed at Munich. But the great point was that Wolfgang was to leave Paris as soon as possible.

In August he had had the pleasure of spending a few delightful days with his friend Bach of London, who was invited to Paris to write an opera, at St. Germain, at the house of Maréchal de Noailles, who possessed an orchestra of his own. Bach's bosom friend, Tendcci, was also there, and for him Wolfgang composed a scena, with pianoforte, oboe, and horn accompaniment. As it was a settled thing that Mozart was to leave Paris, Grimm wished him to be ready to start in eight days' time. This vexed Mozart, for all at once he was seized with the desire of writing six

trios for his Paris publisher, for which he expected to be
well paid.  Meanwhile Grimm pressed him, and even declared himself ready to pay the expenses of his journey as
far as Strasburg.  Mozart was somewhat suspicious of this
friendly offer, but was nevertheless obliged to make use of
it.  Grimm acted in the matter as a practical man, anxious
to acquit himself of all responsibility towards Mozart's
father.  That he did wisely in hastening his protégé's departure is proved by a letter of Mozart to his father from Strasburg, in which he says it is the greatest piece of foolishness
in the world that he should go to Strasburg now, and leave
Paris just at the wrong time.  As events turned out, posterity has every reason to be satisfied with the energy displayed by Grimm and Leopold Mozart.  It was the means
of giving a direction to the genius of the irresolute young
musician, which had the best possible effect upon the development of his art.  Whatever Mozart could learn in Paris
he had learnt.  He had seen, heard, and studied the operas
of Gluck and Grétry ; he had become familiar with the
works of Pergolesi, Piccini, Martini, Sacchini, and other
Italian composers, by means of excellent performances.  He
had, moreover, acquired an intimate knowledge of the peculiarities of the French orchestra.  The effect of the "premier
coup-d'archet " had not been watched by him in vain.  It
was the first step to that brilliant instrumentation of which
he afterwards proved himself a master in " Don Giovanni "
and " Die Zauberflöte."  For the rest, looking to the young
maestro's peculiarities of character, there was no particular
success to be hoped for him in Paris.  His delicate and
poetic temperament was not calculated to impress the Pari-
sians, who, even at that time, were much given to esteem
outward appearance.  Mozart was altogether too noble,
too finely strung for the confusing vortex of the cos-
mopolitan city.  Men like Grimm and Leopold Mozart were
able to perceive this.  Besides, the latter would never have
urged his son to undertake the journey to Paris, had he not
wanted to liberate him from the fetters of his romantic love
affair at Mannheim.

After Wolfgang had made his arrangements with all prac-
ticable speed, and had sent on his mother's effects and other
heavy luggage to Salzburg, he went to take leave of Grimm,

who accompanied him to the coach for Strasburg. Mozart left Paris on the 26th of September. The diligence took five days to reach Strasburg. The means of conveyance chosen by Grimm took eight days to reach Nancy only. Here Mozart left the carriage, apparently by the advice of a German merchant, whose acquaintance he had made on the way, and with whom he engaged to continue the journey to Strasburg. It is surprising to learn that he did not enter Strasburg till the middle of October. What occasioned this delay is not known. On the 17th of October Mozart gave a concert, without help or advice from anybody, which brought in three louis-d'ors, notwithstanding the presence of such a notability as Prince Max of Zweibrücken. A second concert in the theatre was not more profitable. Still he did not lose heart, and in spite of the scanty audience, played a concerto more than he had announced, and even improvised at the conclusion. A third concert on the 31st of October, brought in only one louis-d'or. Such trifling receipts obliged him to borrow money from friends to pursue his journey. On the 6th of November he entered Mannheim in the diligence. His father, who knew that the Webers had removed to Munich, looked upon this excursion as a foolish freak. But Mozart replied, "As I love Mannheim, so also Mannheim loves me."

There was a report that the Elector would again take up his residence at Mannheim, because the Bavarians were too coarse for him. This rumour reawakened in Mozart the longing for a commission to write an opera for Mannheim, especially as influential men in that place were ventilating the idea of establishing a German national opera there. It was a favourite idea of Baron von Gemmingen to employ Mozart for this purpose. The baron had written a "duodrama" entitled "Semiramis," and an opera, "Cora." For the first he wanted Mozart to compose the music. He had already been in treaty with Gluck and Schweitzer about the opera; still, in order to be on the safe side, he applied to Mozart as well. But Mozart declined. He said it was inadvisable to trouble about an opera while one had no singers. His father earnestly urging the continuation of his journey, Mozart now took leave of his Mannheim circle of friends, amongst whom the Cannabichs had been foremost, as before, in cordiality and good-will. He left Mannheim on the 9th of December, and accompanied the imperial prelate of Kaysersheim as far as Munich, where he safely arrived on Christmas Day, after some pleasant days spent at Kaysersheim. Naturally his first meeting with the Webers was a joyful event, and Mozart would not have thought of travelling further if his father had not affectionately but seriously reminded him that the decree confirming his appointment at Salzburg was already four months old. He must not delay longer if the archbishop was not to rescind it. To this Mozart replied calmly, that he was ready to come immediately. The longing of his father and sister to see him again must have been very pleasing to him, for in Aloysia, now become a celebrated singer, he no longer found his old love. So his father was right, after all, in looking upon the friendship of the Webers as a selfish one. Mozart seated himself at the Webers' harpsichord, and sang resignedly, "I leave the girl gladly who cares not for me." Aloysia afterwards married the actor Lange. Mozart could not get over his passion so quickly, and, when at Vienna, considered it fortunate that Aloysia's husband was so jealous that no approach on his part was possible.

On the 8th of January, 1779, however, he composed a grand aria with orchestra for Aloysia, for which he chose words from Gluck's "Alceste." It had an obbligato accompaniment of oboe and bassoon. The aria is worthy of note in this respect, that it is the first dramatic attempt of Mozart in which he made a practical use of the experience he had gained in his visit to Paris. The choice of text, too, is very remarkable, for therein he enters the lists with Gluck and Schweitzer. It was a contest he could successfully sustain, for both in imaginative faculty and dramatic characterization, Mozart here for the first time distances Gluck, whose style, in accordance with dramatic continuity it is true, is much balder. In every respect the aria makes unusual demands on the singer. Its composition gives us an exact idea of Aloysia's capabilities at that time, and we can but wonder at her skill, which was well adapted to fill Mozart with enthusiasm. Nevertheless she seems to have been of a cold and reserved nature. The aria was a farewell. On the 7th of January, the day before its composition, Mozart presented the Electress with the sonatas dedicated to her. She remained with him for half an hour, but nothing was said of the project of an appointment at Munich. Next day he took formal leave of the Webers, and started for home, in company with a merchant of Salzburg—Gschwendtner.

We cannot help being moved in trying to picture to ourselves the meeting between father, son, and daughter after their long separation, and the painful events that had happened in the meantime. The family group thus presented to our imagination is a noble and touching one. Mozart had buried his mother in Paris, in Munich he had buried his first deep passion. To be brief, he brought home with him nothing but disillusionment, and must now bow his neck once more under the old hated yoke. Some diversion from his sad thoughts was created by the advent of the "Bäsle," the daughter of his uncle at Augsburg, who came on a visit. Of the sentiments privately entertained towards him by the archbishop, who had only decided upon recalling him because he was in a measure constrained to do so, Mozart scarcely cared to think. Certainly nothing that was friendly was to be expected on that side. Nor, indeed, was much to be looked for from the conditions of art at Salzburg, and it therefore cost him much, as he himself says, to work there. Meanwhile he composed much instrumental and sacred music. The latter chiefly demonstrates the great progress he had made in the mastery over thematic treatment. In dramatic art, too, he entered upon an interesting sphere, in the composition of the choruses and entr'acte music to Gebler's drama, "King Thamos," which was played by a theatrical company at Salzburg. He also took in hand a German operetta, the text of which had been written by Schachtner, the old and tried friend of the family. It is this operetta, which, all but finished, but left nameless by Mozart, was published by André under the title of "Zaïdé," the name of the heroine. The work was most likely destined for performance at Salzburg, for the operetta is not written for virtuosi, but for singers of moderate capacity. The style of the orchestral music also points to this supposition. Mozart introduced melodrama into this operetta; the same thing had been done previously, and with

great success by Benda for the singers Brandes and Seyler,
in the solo scenas, "Ariadne " and " Medea." Mozart's new
venture is a happy adaptation of Benda's style. Still he does
not seem to have cared much for this species of art, which
does full justice neither to declamation nor music, although
it is, perhaps, in their alternation that its chief charm lies.
Mozart never took "Zaïdé" up again. It was certainly wanting
in the peculiar motives of dramatic effect.

Thus passed in quiet, steady work the year 1779, and the first
half of 1780. In the latter year the master, as now he deserves
to be called, received a summons to write a grand opera for the
carnival of 1781 at Munich. The influence of Raaf and Cannabich had at length prevailed. The subject chosen was the
story of Idomeneus, king of Crete. The court-chaplain of Salzburg, Varesco, was commissioned to supply the libretto.
Being in daily communication with Mozart, he could comply
with all his wishes. The German translation, which afterwards became necessary, was the work of Mozart's friend,
Schachtner, so that Leopold Mozart could exclaim with
patriotic enthusiasm, "It was all by inhabitants of Salzburg, the poetry by the court-chaplain here, Abbate Varesco,
the music by my son, the German translation by Herr
Schachtner." Instructions had been received from Munich
that the French opera, "Idoménée," by Danchet, to
which Campra had composed the music, was to serve as
the groundwork of the new libretto. This opera was first
performed at the Royal Academy of Music, Paris, in 1712,
and was again brought into notice in 1731. The story rests
upon the ancient legend of Idomeneus, king of Crete, who,
returning from the conquest of Troy, is overtaken by a
storm at sea, and, to appease Neptune, makes a vow that
he will sacrifice to the god the first thing that meets him
on his arrival at home. Unhappily, the first person he en-
counters is his son Idamante. To evade the fulfilment of
his vow, the king determines to send his son into exile in a
distant country. But at the moment when the young
prince is preparing to embark, a fearful storm arises,
and the waves roll in a tremendous flood, which devastates
the fields of Crete. The people demand of the king,
through the high-priest, that he shall fulfil his vow, and
name the person destined for sacrifice. Idomeneus names his

son. The sacrifice is prepared. As Idomeneus is about to give his son the fatal blow, in rushes Ilia, the daughter of Priam, who, taken prisoner by Idomeneus, has been sent to Crete, and is loved by Idamante. Ilia announces that she will die instead of her beloved. Suddenly the voice of the god is heard, commanding Idomeneus to resign his throne, and Idamante to reign in his stead, united to Ilia. Idomeneus fulfils the decree of the deity, and the opera concludes with a joyful chorus and a pantomimic action.

The French original does not end so mildly. In it Idomeneus becomes demented, and kills his son, while Ilia falls by her own hand. But the tradition, as established by Metastasio, forbade such a tragic ending to the opera. Varesco certainly endeavoured, by means of certain peculiarities of the French original, to reanimate the scheme of serious opera. But, above all things, he placed the acting more in the foreground than was hitherto customary, the effect of which is a livelier exchange of arias, choruses, and ensembles than is elsewhere to be found in the serious opera of that time. It is characteristic that Varesco has throughout faithfully observed the principle of separating musically each individual situation. Although there are interesting and dramatic passages in "Idomeneo," the librettist has given Mozart no opportunity for musical development of continuous motives. A finale was, therefore, out of the question. Varesco's was not an inventive genius. He was skilful enough to profit by certain advantages possessed by French grand opera, being prompted thereto by the original work lying before him, but here his art came to a standstill. Still "Idomeneo" marks an important epoch in the history of the opera, for the music which Mozart composed to it strikes out quite a new path. The youthful musician, now grown to man's estate, was at least able to show the world that he had not reaped experience in vain in Paris and Mannheim. Moreover, we must ascribe to Mozart's influence on his librettist a series of innovations in the treatment of the book, which had their origin in his earnest desire to lend deeper and more vigorous expression to the music.

At the beginning of November Mozart repaired to Munich with the unfinished score. The archbishop had given him leave of absence for six weeks. Mozart was enthusiastically welcomed to Munich by his old friends from Mannheim, the

Cannabichs, Ramm, Wendling, and Raaff, now quite naturalized inhabitants of Munich. The intendant of the theatre, too, was most courteous. He presented him to the Elector, who cordially expressed his pleasure at seeing Mozart again. When Mozart said he would endeavour to win his Serene Highness's approval, the Elector graciously answered, "Oh, I have no doubt all will go well. A piano piano si va lontano." A reception like this must have been most agreeable to the artist who, in the monotonous and joyless court life of Salzburg, had been accustomed to no such encouragement. Mozart had some trouble with the singers, the castrato Del Prato, and even his friend Raaff. He had to study the whole of Del Prato's part with him, and it was only with difficulty that old Raaff was induced to remain for the rehearsals of the ensembles, for instance, to take part in the splendid quartet. Afterwards, indeed, he changed his mind, and became quite enthusiastic over what at first he could not understand. He was particularly delighted with the arias in the opera composed for himself. Besides the two singers above-named, there were "old" Panzacchi, and Valesi, tried veterans whose bloom was long past. The two female parts were well-filled by Dorothea and Elizabeth Wendling. Both ladies were in raptures with their parts. On the whole, therefore, Leopold Mozart's mistrust of the vocal cast was not justifiable. At the end of November, the first act was rehearsed in full with the greatest success. Notwithstanding that Mozart was suffering from a violent cold, he worked on with the greatest zeal.

His father exhorted him to take care of himself. He also wrote to him that he should think in further composition of the unmusical public, and not forget the so-called "Popolare," which tickles long ears. Mozart replied, "Do not trouble about the 'Popolare,' for in my opera there is music for all sorts of people, those with long ears not excepted." By the middle of December the second act was rehearsed. Old Cannabich and the orchestra grew more and more enthusiastic. One of the next rehearsals took place in presence of the Elector. After the storm, which is certainly one of the most remarkable musical conceptions of the master, the Elector said, laughing, "One would not have thought that there was anything so great in such a little head." Afterwards he said, "I was quite surprised; no music has ever had such an effect on me, it is magnificent." Words such as these in high places, of course, found their way to Salzburg. Leopold Mozart was overjoyed. Of the subterranean voice in the third act, an imitation of the oracle in Gluck's " Alceste," he promised himself great things. Mozart lays particular stress upon the point that only three trombones and two horns, as with Gluck, should play, and that all the rest of the orchestra should be silent, an effect previously made use of by Mozart in the recitative of the high-priest. Here we may seek the germ of an instrumentation which in its perfection is admired at the present day in Richard Wagner's operas.

As already mentioned, a pantomimic ballet was added as a wind up. Mozart received the commission to write the music for this also. He was much pleased at this, although it only gave him extra work ; for as he says, " the music is thus all by *one* master." However, the " cursed " dances gave him much trouble. On the 18th of January, 1781, he was at last able to write, " Laus Deo, at last I have accomplished it !" The first representation was repeatedly put off. At last on the 27th of January, Mozart's birthday, the chief rehearsal took place, and two days later, on the 29th, the first performance. Leopold Mozart had waited for the favourable opportunity of the archbishop's departure for Vienna, to make an excursion with his daughter to Munich. Other Salzburg people, Frau von Robini, the ladies Barisani, and the court-musician Fiala, also came to Munich to witness the first performance of "Idomeneo." The Mozart family, being now all together at Munich for this important occasion, we are deprived of their careful, epistolary accounts. In the Munich " Staatsgelehrten und vermischten Nachrichten," there is a short notice of the first performance of "Idomeneo" which mentions, indeed, the Salzburg origin of the whole opera, but not once the name of Mozart. On the other hand the various scenes painted by Lorenzo Quaglio are one and all enumerated and praised. We have no contemporary account of an opera by whose means a great master first demonstrated to the world the power of his genius, a genius which threatened, for the first time, Gluck's sole empire over the lyric drama.

In the opinion of Oulibicheff, the clever Russian biographer

of Mozart, " Idomeneo " plainly shows to what extent Mozart
deviated from the old serious opera of the French school and of
Gluck. This is only true to a limited extent. As regards dramatic conception, Mozart, like Gluck, leaned towards French
modes of expression. The Italian manner he had so fully assimi-
lated to his own nature, that in certain passages of "Idomeneo"
one may speak of a specially Italian colouring. Italian influences predominated to such an extent in Mozart's early
musical education, that whatever afterwards contributed to its
development was adopted by him less from inclination than
reflection. The fresh, budding life of German poetic art, which
was unfolding almost side by side with the expansion
of Mozart's own genius, had met with little or no notice from
him. Not till his artistic development had reached its highest
point, did he recognize that he was a German. It is true
that the nobler aspects of German thought and feeling
assert themselves in his creations, and " Idomeneo " is
the first example of those compositions in which the great
master's German individuality has impregnated the solid and
finished form of his Italian art. To the character of Ilia
especially, doubly unhappy as being torn from her fatherland,
and as the unfortunate heroine of the love episode, Mozart
has lent a depth of feeling, such as before him Handel alone,
—a still closer prisoner in the fetters of Italian art,—knew
how to impart to his Iole in " Heracles."

The six weeks' leave granted by the archbishop to his
court-organist—now become a celebrated man—had long ex-
pired. But his Grace's departure to Vienna, whither he
had travelled to congratulate the Emperor Joseph on his
accession to the throne, had made it possible for Mozart
without further obstacles to remain on the spot in Munich.
All at once he received an express command to repair instantly to Vienna. On the 12th of March he set out, reached
Vienna on the 16th, and had a room assigned to him by the
archbishop in the house he occupied, "Deutsches Haus" in the
Singerstrasse. Mozart dined with Brunetti and Ceccarelli at
the table of the archbishop's servants. This was not at all to
his taste, especially after the marks of favour and distinction
he had just been receiving from the Elector of Bavaria and
the aristocracy of Munich. In the first letter he writes to
his father, he begins to pour forth his indignation. The arch-

bishop made Mozart play on various occasions at the houses of Prince Gallitzin, of his father the old Prince Colloredo, and elsewhere, without being particularly generous in recompensing his extraordinary performances. Besides, Mozart's indignation was justifiable, for on one of these evenings he had been invited to the house of the Countess Thun, when the emperor was present, and when each artist who assisted received fifteen ducats. Of course Mozart had to forego this honour and profit. The archbishop, moreover, would not allow Mozart to play in public. Nevertheless he could not withhold his assent to Mozart's playing for the "Society of Musicians," as this was for a benevolent object. The concert took place on the 3rd of April, and Mozart had an enormous success. What brilliant prospects might have opened for him if he could have given a concert of his own! But the archbishop would not permit it; he even wanted to send his musicians back to Salzburg. In that case all hope of a good opening for the future would have been at an end. So Mozart thought of remaining in Vienna even without the consent of his master. A few good pupils would procure him the wherewithal to live. However, the departure was delayed. Mozart's irritation increased from day to day.

At the beginning of May it was announced to him that he must vacate his room, and instantly take his departure. He had an audience of the archbishop who grossly insulted him, assailed him with abuse, and showed him the door, saying, "I will have nothing more to do with such a miserable knave!" To this Mozart answered, "And I, too, will have nothing more to do with you!" "Then, go!" replied the archbishop. His Grace's ill-humour is easily explained. He had come to Vienna to ingratiate himself with the emperor; but the latter took little notice of him, and did not even once invite him to Laxenburg. The day after his audience, Mozart formally applied for his dismissal. His father did not agree with him, and endeavoured by his earnest remonstrances to dissuade his son from carrying out his resolution. However, Mozart stood firm; he was acting in full consciousness of the great wrong done to him by the archbishop for years past; his honour he felt had been assailed, and he became even more resolved when he found that he had been calumniated to his father, on account of his bad associations. "I hate the archbishop even to madness!" This is the refrain of his bitter complaints. His Grace had supposed that Leopold Mozart would bring his son to his senses, and make him return to his duty. Count Arco, the chamberlain, had received a letter from Leopold Mozart on the subject, and invited Mozart to a friendly interview. But Mozart still stood firm. Several petitions for discharge never reached the archbishop, for those who surrounded his Grace feared to mention the subject. On the 8th of June, Mozart wanted to present a new petition for discharge, in person. In the antechamber he found Count Arco, who loaded him with the coarsest abuse, and thrust him from the door with a kick. Nothing remained for Mozart but to consider the business as settled. Whether or not the archbishop had ordered this disgraceful treatment is not known. But it is certain that the servant acted in the spirit of his master, whose name is thereby covered with dishonour for all time. Mozart wanted to write a threatening letter to Count Arco. His father endeavoured to appease him. Mozart answered, "I can only consult my reason and my heart, to do what is just and right." At last he calmed down, and relinquished his intentions against Count Arco. And so ended the vassalage of Mozart to the Archbishop of Salzburg.

Compelled to leave the room granted to him by the archbishop, Mozart found admission into the Weber family, who lived in a house called "Auge Gottes," in the Petersplatz. The Webers had left Munich in the year 1780.

Aloysia was engaged at the National Theatre in Vienna by recommendation of Count Hardeck. Here she made her *début* in the part of the "Rosenmädchen von Salency," with considerable success, and thus early and brilliantly justified the expectations of her future career which Mozart's acute perception had made him express to his father. With Aloysia, the whole family had removed to Vienna, where, in the following year, old Weber died. Aloysia married the court actor Lange. So the mother lived with her three other daughters Josepha (afterwards Hofer), Sophie (afterwards Haibl), and Constance in tolerably poor circumstances, depending chiefly on the charitable aid of her now famous daughter Aloysia, who drew the highest salary among her comrades of the National Theatre. Madame Weber was glad to be able to underlet part of her dwelling, and Mozart was doubly agreeable to her as an inmate. But when Leopold Mozart was informed of this new association with the Webers, he would hear nothing of it. He desired that Wolfgang should choose another lodging, so much the more, as evil tongues had spread a report in Salzburg that Mozart would marry one of the daughters. To this Mozart replied on the 25th of July, that he had long since wished to move to another lodging, because of people's chatter. There was no question of his falling in love, and marriage was the very last thing he thought of just then. "I am beginning to live for the first time."

These few words exactly indicate the frame of mind of the artist freed from the archiepiscopal yoke. He adds mischievously in the course of the letter, "If I were obliged to marry all with whom I have joked, I might easily have a hundred wives." Meanwhile the association was not without its dangers to his susceptible heart, as is proved by the circumstance that in the autograph copy of one of his pianoforte sonatas, composed at the time, the names of Sophie and Constance are written over particularly expressive passages. Notwithstanding that Meszmer, his old friend in the Landstrasse, offered him a lodging, he refused it, nominally because Rhigini lived there, with whom he had no sympathy. The Aurnhammer family, too, whose daughter Josepha was esteemed one of the first pianists of the day, wished to have Mozart with them. Mozart declined, although he enjoyed a friendly inter-course with them. People soon began to tease him, and said he was going to marry the "stout young lady." In September he at last complied with his father's wish, and moved to a new lodging on the Graben, which pleased him but little. It was therefore no wonder that the desire arose within him for a home of his own; all the more when people's talk pictured him in intimate relations with the Weber family. Out of this grew his inclination for Constance Weber, which was responded to on her side. In a word, the young people fell in love with each other. On the 15th of December Mozart told his father of his intention to marry Constance. He described her as the one who took upon herself the whole management of the house —a perfect housewife, with the best heart in the world. " I love her, and she loves me from the heart ; tell me if I can wish for a better wife "—the letter culminates in this joyous cry. His father knew of the affair from hearsay before the letter came. He even knew further, that Wolfgang had given a written promise of marriage. The guardian of Weber's children, Johannes Thorwarth, inspector of the theatrical wardrobe, had been prejudiced against Mozart by mischief-makers. He asserted that Mozart had no settled income, that in the end Constance would be left unprovided for. In an interview which Mozart had with him concerning his betrothal and marriage, the guardian demanded of Constance's mother, that she should forbid Mozart the house, and as she did not do this, he prohibited Mozart from all communication with the Webers until he should have declared himself in writing. He, therefore, signed a document, by which he bound himself to marry Constance within three years, or "in the event of such an impossibility happening as that he should alter his mind," to pay her a yearly sum of three hundred florins. The guardian, contented with this, having gone away, Constance, " heavenly girl," tore up the paper, and fell upon Mozart's neck, exclaiming, " Dear Mozart, I need no written assurance from you ; I believe your word ! "

Although Mozart had no fixed appointment, his stay in Vienna was not prospectless. Ladies in high circles— for instance, the Countess Rumbeck née Cobenzl, who for a long time was his pupil, the Countess Thun, and the Baroness Waldstätten—interested themselves for him. Friends like these ensured him popularity as a performer on the pianoforte, and this popularity enabled him to give frequent and very well-attended concerts, of which we shall presently speak. But what was still more to his advantage was the favour he enjoyed with the chief intendant of the Imperial Theatre, Count Rosenberg, through the recommendation of the inspector of theatres, Stephanie. Count Rosenberg had commissioned Schröder, "the excellent actor," to procure a good libretto for Mozart. Stephanie, as official poet attached to the theatre, was now desired to put himself in communication with Mozart.

On the 1st of August Mozart informed his father that he

had received an excellent libretto with a Turkish subject, "Belmonte and Constance, or the Elopement from the Seraglio," which was to be ready for representation in the middle of September  He must therefore set to work with all haste. About that time the visit of the Russian Grand Duke Paul and his duchess was expected. If it were possible for the new opera to be performed at these festivities, Mozart hoped he might rise high in the favour of the Emperor Joseph, and of Count Rosenberg. The first act was finished by the 22nd of August. Then came the news that the Grand Duke would not be in Vienna before November. Mozart was glad to be able to complete his opera "with more deliberation." He also wanted Stephanie during September to give a more dramatic character to the libretto, which was originally written by Bretzner; and this Stephanie did for him. In the meantime Gluck and his adherents carried their point, which was that "Iphigenia in Tauris" in German, and "Alceste" in Italian, should be performed by the singers of the German opera in honour of the Grand Ducal visit, although the Emperor had no particular sympathy either with Gluck or Gluck's favourite singer, Bernasconi. Under these circumstances Mozart had to give up his hope of seeing "Idomeneo," with German words, speedily performed. On the 21st of November the Grand Duke arrived. On the 27th Mozart wrote resigned, "To-morrow 'Alceste' will be at Schönbrunn; I have been looking over the Russian favourite airs, so as to be able to play variations on them." Besides the Russian Grand Duke, other distinguished guests arrived at the imperial court, among them the Duke of Würtemberg with his consort, the Princess Elizabeth, and Prince Ferdinand of Würtemberg. The princess was the bride of the Archduke Franz, and was to finish her education at Vienna. Mozart hoped, through the interest of the Archduke Maximilian, who was then also at Vienna, to obtain the tuition of the princess. However, the Emperor Joseph desired that Salieri, his capellmeister, should teach music to the Princess Elizabeth, on account of his knowledge of the Italian art of singing.

Mozart was only known to the Emperor as a player on the pianoforte, and soon an opportunity occurred to distinguish him specially. On the 24th of December Mozart played in a musical contest with Clementi at court. The

Emperor Joseph took pleasure in such exhibitions. After the two musicians had complimented each other sufficiently, the Emperor desired Clementi to begin:—"La Santa Chiesa Cattolica! because he is a Roman." Clementi played the sonata, the allegro theme of which is very similar to the principal motive of the overture to "Die Zauberflöte." The Emperor then said to Mozart, "Allons, straight on!" Both musicians were, of course, much applauded. Afterwards the emperor asked Dittersdorf how Mozart pleased him. "As he must please every connoisseur," was the answer. "Have you heard Clementi, too?" continued the Emperor. "Some place him before Mozart, and Greybig is at the head of these. What is your opinion on the matter? Tell me freely." Dittersdorf replied, "Mere art prevails in Clementi's playing, but in Mozart's both art and taste." Whereupon the Emperor observed, "That is just what I said. Clementi himself was full of enthusiasm for Mozart's playing, while Mozart could only say of Clementi that he was a good mechanician."

Meanwhile there was not much talk of Mozart's comic opera. At Easter it was to be given, but the second act was not finished till the 7th of May, and the first rehearsal did not take place till the beginning of June. Mozart had many opponents, nor was Salieri very favourably disposed towards him, and hence it happened that an insignificant musician, Summerer, was proposed by him as a teacher for the Princess Elizabeth. In the opinion of contemporaries Salieri was much too politic openly to display his animosity. He was clever enough to see that in Mozart a rival was growing up, who might become dangerous to his own importance and renown. The Emperor's favour continued unalterably his, and, with the help of the Emperor's valet, Strack, who had great influence with his master, he managed to keep off Mozart's influence from the Emperor's private musical entertainments, which took place almost every evening before the theatre. It is, therefore, not to be wondered at that the Emperor, although he recognized Mozart's worth, actually did nothing to improve his outward circumstances. In one respect only did he show his good-will to Mozart. This was in giving an express command for the performance of his comic opera.

The "Entführung aus dem Serail" was represented

for the first time on the 16th of July, 1782. Its success was extraordinary, and several numbers were encored. Nevertheless the Emperor said to Mozart, "Too fine for our ears, my dear Mozart, and a great deal too many notes." To which Mozart replied, "Exactly as many notes as are necessary, your Majesty." The opera was performed sixteen times in the course of the year, and the Russian Grand Duke heard it when he returned to Vienna at the beginning of October. While Dittersdorf was echoing the Emperor's opinion that the accompaniment overpowered the singers, Gluck was full of compliments for the composer. Wherever the opera was performed the same success attended it, and Goethe's opinion that it excelled every other was by no means exaggerated. It was the foundation of German opera, and thus realized the Emperor Joseph's wish. Henceforth German opera not only might but must be talked of. A free use of every resource afforded by the arts of singing and orchestration for the expression of sentiment in music, without any limitations excepting such as are founded on the essence of music and dramatic characterization,—this is the great feat accomplished by Mozart in the " Entführung aus dem Serail." It is true he had the assistance of the select band of artists at that time employed at the National Theatre in Vienna ; the names of Adamberger and Fischer, for whom Mozart in a measure invented the part of Osmin, and the ladies Cavalieri and Teyber were amongst the most celebrated of the German opera. Carl Maria von Weber has left us his opinion as enthusiastic as it is decisive upon the " Entführung." " I am bold to express my belief," he writes, "that in the ' Entführung' Mozart's artistic experience has reached maturity, and after that only experience of the world could lead him further. Of operas like ' Figaro ' and ' Don Giovanni' the world was entitled to expect from him many another. An ' Entführung' he could not have written again with the best of wills. I think I see in it what the happy years of youth are to every man, the youth whose time of bloom he can never get back again, and by the eradication of whose defects, charms as great are irretrievably lost."

Mozart wrote the " Entführung" during the time of his engagement, the stormy commencement of which has been spoken of above. The success of his opera, and the favour which the master found as a performer on the piano-forte, formed the bright spots, in this time of trial, for both the lovers. Leopold Mozart could not be induced to alter his opinion of his son's intended marriage. He was persuaded that on Constance's side the deciding motives were selfish. Mozart and Constance sought, through his sister Marianne, to influence the father in their favour. But to no purpose; and intercourse on the side of the Salzburg family was limited to formalities. Added to this was the ill-temper of Frau Weber, which made life in her mother's house unbearable to the poor girl. Had the Emperor, who interested himself in Mozart's marriage, at that time exerted himself actively, and afforded the young musician a settled source of income, the grievous circumstances of the household about to be established might have been avoided. Whilst under such conditions Mozart's relations with Frau Weber grew more and more unpleasant, and a breach might possibly have been the consequence, the aspect of affairs suddenly changed, owing to the intervention of a friend of Mozart's, the Baroness Waldstätten, who, towards the end of July, took Constance altogether into her house. As, however, Frau Weber made efforts to regain possession of her daughter, there was nothing left but to marry the young couple as quickly as might be, and to this the guardian agreed. Mozart several times earnestly entreated for his father's consent.

Although this was wanting, the baroness managed to overcome all formalities, and on the 4th of August, 1782, the marriage took place in the Church of St. Stephen. The day after the wedding the expected letter of consent from Leopold Mozart and Marianne arrived; Frau Weber, and her youngest daughter Sophie too, had taken part in the ceremony. "When we were joined together," writes Mozart to his father, "my wife and I, too, began to weep; upon which every one, even the priest, was moved, and all who witnessed our emotion wept." The affection of the young couple was sincere and hearty, and this is con-firmed in the most positive manner by several contempo-raries, especially by Professor Niemetschek, of Prague. But their love for each other, deep and mutual as it was, was the only, though certainly the best, possession which the bridal pair could bring into their new condition of life. The "Entführung aus dem Auge Gottes," as Mozart playfully called his marriage, because the house in which his mother-in-law Frau Weber dwelt was called "Zum Auge Gottes," had for its immediate consequence that Leopold Mozart solemnly declared to his son and daughter-in-law that they must not reckon, either now or in the future, upon receiving any support from him. To this Mozart replied that the friendship and love of Constance for him was so great that she would willingly sacrifice her whole future life to his fate. The first dwelling-place of Mozart and his bride was in the "Grosshaupt" House, on the great bridge, now Wipplingerstrasse, at the sign of the "Rothe Säbel" (red sabre).

Constance was distinguished neither by talents nor education. Her intellectual influence upon Mozart was not important. Probably she had not the least suspicion of his greatness, which, indeed, was at that time recognized by but very few of his contemporaries. However, Mozart himself praised her common sense. She was, moreover, not wanting in musical gifts. She could play tolerably on the pianoforte, and sang very prettily, particularly at sight, so that Mozart was accustomed to try new compositions with her. It is interesting to know that she took great delight in the fugues of Handel and Bach, and animated Mozart to write down fugues, which he improvised at the piano. Consequently Mozart found in his wife appreciation for his art, and, fortunately, a judicious appreciation, which was in no way prejudicial to his productive power. While Mozart worked, his wife sat by him and related to him legends and children's tales to his great content. Unhappily Constance became delicate from severe confinements, and this was a heavy trial for the family. On the other hand it proved the goodness of Mozart's heart, for he took care of his wife in the tenderest manner. Trials only served to knit yet closer their affectionate relations to each other. Nor were these relations endangered even by the slight breaches of conjugal fidelity of which Mozart was guilty. This "chambermaids' tattle," as Frau Constance expressed it, has unfortunately been much exaggerated in passing from mouth to mouth of so many narrators, and Mozart's character has in consequence been frequently painted as fickle and unsteady. How little in accordance with the reality this is, we may see by the following passage in a letter to his friend Jacquin. He writes:—" Is not the pleasure of a fickle, fleeting passion as far removed from the bliss which a true, reasonable love procures as earth is from heaven? You will indeed, I hope, thank me often in your heart for my advice." Whatever has been told of Mozart's extravagance is altogether exaggerated. The many pecuniary embarrassments in which he was involved from the outset of his married life, may have given rise to imputations on his character of the kind referred to. When old Mozart visited his son in Vienna in 1785, he had an opportunity of convincing himself that the housekeeping, as far as eating and drinking were concerned, was in the highest degree economical. Six months after the marriage the young couple found themselves in the utmost need, out of which their faithful friend the Baroness Waldstätten helped them.

Unfortunately the hopes of obtaining some fixed appointment which Mozart had rested upon the success of the "Entführung," were doomed to disappointment. As has been said, he did not even obtain the tuition of the Princess Elizabeth of Würtemberg. So that only a fortnight after his marriage he began to entertain the design of leaving Vienna. "The gentlemen of Vienna" (by which is chiefly meant the Emperor), he writes to his father, "must not think that my only aim of existence is Vienna. There is no monarch in the world I would rather serve than the Emperor, but I will not beg for employment. I believe my standing is such that at any court I could make a reputation. If Germany, my beloved fatherland, of which, as you know, I am proud, will not take me up, France or England must in God's name, become the richer by a clever German—and that to the shame of the German nation. You are well aware that in nearly every art those who have excelled were always Germans. But where did they obtain fame and fortune? Certainly not in Germany. Gluck even—has Germany made him a great man? The Countess Thun, Count Zichy, Baron van Swieten, and even Prince Kaunitz, are dissatisfied with the Emperor because he does not set more value on people of talent, and lets them leave his dominions. The latter said lately, speaking of me, to the Archduke Maximilian, that such men only came into the world once in every century, and should not be driven out of Germany, especially if one was so fortunate as actually to possess them in the capital."

Mozart had indeed turned his attention to France and England, and had even diligently studied French and English. His father was very averse to the idea, and pressed into his service the influence of the Baroness Waldstätten to dissuade Mozart from his purpose. Mozart gave way, unfortunately, for the expected appointment failed to come ; so that the only income which he had to depend on was that derived from the lessons he gave, and from his concerts. During his engagement Mozart had gone into partnership with a man named Martin, a native of Ratisbon and a friend of Bullinger, who in the winter of 1781-2 had given very successful concerts in the "Mehlgrube," a concert-room in the Mehlmarkt (flour-market). Martin had obtained the Emperor Joseph's permission to give twelve concerts in the Augarten, and four grand evening musical entertainments in the finest squares of Vienna. In these Mozart took part, and played for the first time on the 26th of May, in the Augarten, a large hall in the Augarten Park, which the Emperor Joseph had given up for the general use of the public in 1775. The first concert was a brilliant success, but afterwards report is silent as to the result of the undertaking, which probably did not come up to the expectations formed of it. In the following Lent, 1783, however, Mozart had an important success at a concert which he gave. He also assisted at a concert given by his sister-in-law, Aloysia Lange, on the 11th of March, and met with great approval from Gluck, who was present. On the 22nd of March he gave an "academy" of his own in the theatre, at which only his own compositions were performed. The Emperor was present, and the proceeds amounted to 1600 florins.

It had long been Mozart's wish to introduce his wife to his father and sister. Various obstacles, in particular Constance's state of health, had repeatedly prevented an interchange of visits. At the beginning of the year he and his wife had removed to Burg's House, in the Judenplatz. On the 17th of June Karl Leopold Mozart was born, and at the end of July the husband and wife set out on a journey to Salzburg. Mozart brought with him to Salzburg, completed, the greater part of a mass which he had made a vow to compose, in case he should bring Constance as his wife to Salzburg. It was performed on the 25th of August, in the Church of St. Peter, Constance singing the soprano part.

That the family lived in the greatest harmony during the visit is proved by the fact that the young couple prolonged their stay till the 27th of October. During this time, Mozart composed for old Michael Haydn, who was recovering from a severe illness, two chamber duets for violin and viola, which the archbishop had peremptorily demanded, even threatening Haydn with the loss of his salary in case of non-compliance. It was at this time too that Mozart made the acquaintance of the blind pianist, Maria Theresa Paradis, for whom next year he composed a concerto. If very cordial relations were not established between Leopold Mozart and Marianne on the one hand, and Constance on the other, the Salzburgers had at any rate an opportunity of convincing themselves of the intimate affection which subsisted between husband and wife. On their return to Vienna they remained a few days at Lintz, on a visit to the Thun family. On the 4th of November Mozart gave an "academy," for which occasion he composed in all haste a symphony, which was performed. It was the C major symphony (Koechel, 425), and afforded brilliant proof of the progress made by Mozart in the art of instrumentation by his composing the "Entführung." There is a drawing by Mozart made during these happy days at Lintz representing an Ecce Homo. It has the words, "Linz, 13th November, 1783, dedié à Mme. Mozart son épouse;" and was preserved by Constance as a proof that Mozart had a talent for drawing as well as for music.

In the meantime German opera was given up in Vienna, and through Salieri's influence Italian opera was once more introduced. The best singers, Lange, Cavalieri, Teyber, and even Bernasconi went over to Italian opera, and in December, 1783, "Iphigenia in Tauris" was produced in Italian. Unfortunately the distinguished bass, Fischer, was dismissed, but a bass-buffo of the first rank, Benucci, was engaged in his stead. In addition to the Germans, Adamberger, Saal, and Rupprecht, distinguished foreign singers were also engaged.

These were Mandini, Buzzani, Pugnetti, and the tenor, Michael Kelly, who frequently came in contact with Mozart. The list was, moreover, strengthened by the ladies, Nancy Storace and Mandini; and, later, by the famous Celestine Cottellini. The Italian opera (opera-buffa) had an extraordinary success. Naturally Mozart gained new suggestions from it, as, indeed, he had also done from his journey to Lintz. In order to be busy himself with opera-buffa, he applied, through his father's mediation, to Varesco, of Salzburg. On his arrival in Salzburg he found Varesco prepared with the design of a libretto rich in absurdities, " Oca del Cairo," the composition of which Mozart took in hand while at Salzburg, and continued immediately upon his return to Vienna. However, he found that the substance of the book must undergo alterations, and at length, towards the close of the year, he became convinced that it was radically at fault, and so left it alone, although he had almost completely sketched it out. The libretto lately has been revised in Paris by Victor Wilder, the sketches left by Mozart being completed by Charles Constantin, and the work has been produced in Paris, Vienna, Berlin, and London, in the latter city at Drury Lane, on the 12th of May, 1870.

In 1784 Mozart was busy with a new opera-buffa, " Lo sposo deluso," which he likewise soon abandoned. We may consider these works as preparatory to " Figaro." In Lent he arranged three concerts in a fine room belonging to the bookseller Trattnern. He obtained a hundred and seventy-four subscribers, belonging to the most aristocratic circles in Vienna. At the beginning of April he arranged two grand "academies" in the theatre, at which the beautiful quintet for piano and wind instruments was given. Of this quintet Mozart says, "I consider it the best I have yet written in my life." Besides performing at his own concerts, Mozart played during Lent five times at Prince Gallitzin's, nine times at Count Johann Esterhazy's, and three times at the concerts of the pianoforte teacher, Richter. We see from this list of concerts how anxious Mozart was to increase his popularity as an executant. About this time he wrote for the lady-violinist, Regina Strinasacchi, of Ostiglia, near Mantua, who was passing through Vienna on a tour, a sonata (Koechel, 454) which he played with her at an " academy" on the 24th of April. The sonata was not ready in time, and the violinist had much trouble to get her part from Mozart the evening before the concert. They played it at the concert without rehearsal. The Emperor Joseph, looking through his glass, fancied he perceived that Mozart had no notes in front of him, and sent for him to his box, with a request that he would bring the sonata with him. But there was only an empty music-book. Mozart had played the sonata from memory, and had only hastily sketched the violin part. It was at this time that he began to busy himself with the six great quartets, which he afterwards dedicated to Haydn. It is characteristic of Mozart's goodwill to other artists that, speaking of the quartets by Pleyel which appeared at the same time, he said it was worth while to become acquainted with them. "Well and fortunate for music if Pleyel, in his time, is able to replace Haydn to us." The year passed away in composition, music-lessons, and social intercourse with many friends of art. To his sister Marianne, he wrote once, that she was to send him his old oratorio, " Betulia Liberata ;" he wished to recompose it for the Society of Musicians, and wanted to make use of the earlier setting. But this came to nothing. At the end of August Marianne Mozart married Joh. Bapt. Berchthold, of Sonnenburg, Baron of the Empire, Aulic Counsellor at Salzburg, and administrator of the chapter of St. Gilgen.

Mozart had often expressed his desire that his father should come to Vienna, and at last Leopold could no longer withstand his son's request. On the 10th of February, 1785, he arrived in Vienna, and on the following day had the pleasure of being present at the first subscription concert given by Mozart in the "Mehlgrube," with a hundred and fifty subscribers. At an "academy" which he gave in the theatre, and which was a splendid success, his father writes to Marianne that Wolfgang took five hundred and fifty-nine florins. On the occasion of Mdme. Laschi's concert, Mozart, having played the concerto composed by him for the blind pianist Paradis, the emperor complimented him, hat in hand, and called out, "Bravo, Mozart!" It was a great delight to the old man to relate all this to his daughter. Leopold Mozart had, moreover, the elder Haydn's opinion of his son from his own mouth, an opinion which must have reconcilod him to all that had gone before. Mozart had instituted quartet entertainments in his roomy lodgings in the Camesina House in the Schulerstrasse, whither he had moved at Michaelmas, 1784. Soon after his father's arrival he invited Joseph Haydn and both the Barons Todi to hear his new quartets. Haydn himself played the first violin, Dittersdorf the second, Mozart the viola, and Vanhal the violoncello. After they had played the three quartets Haydn took the old man aside, and said to him, " I tell you, by God, and as an honest man, that I acknowledge your son to be the greatest composer of whom I have ever heard ; he has taste, and possesses the most thorough knowledge of composition." Leopold Mozart could appreciate the value of Haydn's opinion.

From this time his son rose considerably in his estimation, and obtained so much influence over him, that Leopold let himself be persuaded to join the Freemasons, to which brotherhood Mozart had for some time belonged: By means of the secret bond of Freemasonry the great minds of the latter half of the eighteenth century, Frederick the Great, Lessing, and Wieland, had actively sought to educate mankind to the principle of co-operation. The movement, which was at its height in Vienna just when Mozart took up his permanent abode there, was one he could not avoid joining, filled with hatred, too, as he was against the clergy, because the archbishop had behaved badly to his father, and, indeed, to all his dependants. Mozart was a member of the lodge " Zur gekrönten Hoffnung." Freemasonry rapidly grew, and became the fashion. The brethren, whether in high or low positions in life, actively supported each other. The spirit of charity was certainly promoted by it. When, in 1785, the Emperor Joseph decreed the amalgamation of the eight lodges of Vienna into three, and officially recognized the order, many influential members withdrew. Mozart, on the other hand, continued to be actively interested in it to the end of his life, and fostered the benevolent tendencies of the secret craft. He even wanted to found a new society, " Zur Grotte," the rules of which he himself drew up. It was part of his character to entertain and cherish real heartfelt friendship. As a proof we have but to think of Pater Johaunes of Seeon, of Thomas Linley, and of Bullinger, to whom was added in Vienna Gottfried von Jacquin, son of the celebrated botanist, and a great enthusiast for music. The house of the Jacquins, in the Landstrasse, was the resort of the cultivated world, who found enjoyment in serious and pleasant conversation. Mozart's relations with this intellectually distinguished family were most intimate. It is easy of comprehension that Mozart, to whom friendships such as these were a necessity, should feel attracted by the tenets of the Freemasons, who aspired to universal brotherhood. Moreover, there was the hostile attitude which Freemasonry assumed towards monasticism and the priesthood, with which Mozart completely sympathized. This, indeed, was also the bridge over which his father willingly stepped into the precincts of the order. Leopold was careful to make Marianne mark the difference between true self-denying Christianity and bigotry. In this he clearly had in view the practical Christianity of Freemasonry. As to Mozart himself, intimate association with the many distinguished men among his masonic brethren proved a source of intellectual enjoyment, than which nothing more profitable and welcome after the narrowness and retirement of his Salzburg life could have fallen to his lot. In the funeral oration delivered after Mozart's death it was expressly stated that he was a zealous adherent of the order. "Love for his brethren, sociability, concord in a good cause, charity, a genuine and fervent feeling of pleasure when he could make his talents useful to one of the brethren—such were the chief features of his character." These words involuntarily remind us of the words of the priests in "Die Zauberflöte," inquiring into the character of Tamino, whom Sarastro wishes to introduce into the Temple of Prudence. As music played a legitimate part in masonic ceremonies, Mozart found a new sphere for the employment of his beautiful inspiration. Shortly before his father's departure on the 20th of April, 1785, he had his cantata, "Maurer Freude," performed. The occasion was a feast given in honour of the chemist Born, an old friend of Mozart, and Leopold Mozart was present.

Soon after, in July, Mozart composed the "Masonic Funeral Music on the Deaths of Brothers Mecklenburg and Esterhazy," one of the most solemn and expressive, and, at the same time, sonorously beautiful pieces which the entire range of music can show. The music of the piece—a short adagio—is grouped round a *cantus firmus*, which occurs in old antiphons, as, for instance, the Penitential Psalm. The freedom of the contrapuntal treatment is admirable. The enthusiasm of Mozart for the order of Freemasons becomes more explicable by a circumstance which estranged him from his nearest colleagues. This circumstance was as follows. Mozart had composed for the Society of Musicians, also a charitable association which had for its object the succour of the widows and orphans of musicians, the cantata "Davidde Penitente," partly taken from the mass composed by him for Salzburg. The cantata was produced on the 13th and 15th of March, 1785. He had also, as already stated, frequently taken part in the concerts of the society. When he applied for admission into the society, on the 11th of February, at the same time remarking that he would produce his certificate of baptism subsequently, the request remained unanswered. After the appearance of the cantata Mozart repeated his request, and on the 24th of August received for answer : "If the certificate of baptism has been sent, further information will be given." There the matter rested. Mozart, who probably felt hurt, did not become a member of the society for which he had done so much. It is quite intelligible that he should have clung all the more closely to his masonic brethren after the ungracious treatment he had met with from his colleagues.

An inducement to new dramatic compositions was not wanting at this period. Anton Klein, author of the libretto of "Gunther von Schwartzburg," sent Mozart a book for an opera entitled "Rudolph von Habsburg." Mozart, however, would not set to work upon the music until he saw a surer prospect of the opera being put upon the stage. Although there was again a desire for German opera, and the Kärnthnerthor-theatre had been prepared for its performance, we hear nothing more of "Rudolph von Habsburg." Strange to say, Mozart was not employed as a composer of German opera. Altogether it seemed as if the Emperor Joseph had forgotten his existence. Not till his Imperial Majesty was in want of a vaudeville to be played by German and Italian singers for a performance in the Orangery at

Schönbrunn, was Mozart remembered. It was to this that Stephanie's occasional piece, "Der Schauspiel Director," with music by Mozart, owed its production, on the 6th of February, 1786. Soon after, on the 11th of February, a second performance was given in the Kärnthnerthor-theatre, but with very moderate success, for the piece left much to be desired; and the music, consisting only of few numbers, could not atone for its defects. However, the year 1785 had not drawn to its close before things had taken a favourable turn for Mozart and for his art. The "tool of fate" in this case was a dramatic writer established in Vienna by Salieri's influence—Lorenzo Da Ponte—who was born at Ceneda, in the territory of the Republic of Venice, 1749, and died at New York, 1838. Salieri had no luck with Da Ponte's first opera, "Il ricco d'un giorno," and consequently declared he would never again compose a single verse of Da Ponte's. Da Ponte, who was a man of talent, saw his position threatened, especially as a rival had sprung up for him, in the person of the poet Casti, who was favoured by Salieri and the Intendant, Count Rosenberg, and who was eager to supplant him by all imaginable devices. He could not help reflecting that the dispute as to the worth of the libretto might with advantage be transferred to the province of the music, and that before all things it was desirable to obtain good composers. With Vincenzio Martin he had some success, but he was less fortunate with Gazzaniga and Righini. Then he became acquainted with Mozart, through Baron Wezlar, a man of artistic tastes. At the house of this Mæcenas, the following plan was discussed. Da Ponte was to furnish Mozart with a libretto, for which Wezlar was to pay. If its representation was impossible in Vienna, then care should be taken that it should appear in London or Paris. Da Ponte, however, would not agree to this proposal; but, as luck would have it, he fell in with Mozart's desire that he should remodel, for the operatic stage, Beaumarchais' comedy "Le mariage de Figaro," which had recently appeared in Paris, and of which all the world was talking.

At the beginning of November, 1785, Mozart set to work with the utmost diligence, and, according to Da Ponte's report, completed his score in six weeks, that is, at the beginning of the new year (1786). Da Ponte went straight to the

Emperor with the finished work, but his Majesty did not enter into the affair very heartily, because he had no great opinion of Mozart's dramatic talent, and also because he had forbidden the performance of Beaumarchais' piece. Still he allowed Mozart to bring him the score, and to play some of it to him, after which he immediately decided on accepting it.

Of course matters did not progress without intrigues on the part of Casti and Count Rosenberg. But the Emperor was more than once present at the rehearsals; and, on the 1st of May, 1786, this "musical comedy" *par excellence* was put upon the stage. The singer Kelly, who performed in it, has given us the following remarkable account of its success in his "Reminiscences:"—"Never was anything more complete than the triumph of Mozart and his 'Nozze di Figaro,' to which numerous overflowing audiences bore witness. Even at the full band rehearsal all present were roused to enthusiasm; and when Benucci came to the fine passage, 'Cherubino, alla vittoria alla gloria militar,' which he gave with stentorian lungs, the effect was electric, for the whole of the performers on the stage, and those in the orchestra, vociferated 'Bravo! Bravo, Maestro! Viva! viva! grande Mozart!' And Mozart? I never shall forget his little countenance when lighted up with the glowing rays of genius; it is as impossible to describe it, as it would be to paint sunbeams." Many pieces had to be repeated. The Emperor found it necessary to forbid the encores. Once at rehearsal he said to the singers that he believed in this he had done them a service; and when they bowed gracefully, and assented, Mozart stepped forward and said, "Do not believe it, your Majesty. They all like to have an encore. I, at least can certainly say so for my part." Whereupon the Emperor laughed. The enormous success of "Figaro" was somewhat diminished by intrigues. In its first year it was performed nine times. But on the 17th of November Martin's "Cosa rara" obtained an incredible success, and completely supplanted "Figaro." The cast of "Figaro" was as follows:—The Count, Signor Mandini; the Countess, Signora Laschi; Susanna, Signora Storace; Figaro, Signor Benucci; Cherubino, Signora Bussani; Basilio and Curzio, Signor Kelly. This list shows that none of the German singers were engaged for "Figaro." The greatest feat achieved in "Figaro" was the artistic elaboration of the finales, upon which modern opera is evidently founded. These finales, on the other hand, are only a practical consequence of the fundamental principle of dramatic art as generally laid down by Mozart. Its essence is nothing but truth of characterization. Generally speaking the result of this principle, which was till then almost unknown, was to create a kind of ideal halo round all the situations of "Figaro," equivocal as they often are. The whole is transformed, as it were, by the delicate and noble spirit which asserts itself all through. There is an almost antique joy of existence, combined with the growth of noblest sentiment, in Mozart music. Rossini is right when, for this reason, he calls "Figaro" a real "dramma giocoso." And the psychology of this work is as easy of comprehension, as on the other hand its depth is unfathomable. Every fresh hearing brings with it the delight of discovering new beauties in a work whose geniality and warmth act instantly like a charm. Otto Jahn, the profound Hellenic scholar, says of "Figaro," that this is the genuine eternal art which makes us free and happy.

So much the more sad is it that Mozart's circumstances, after his creating this masterpiece, were in no way improved. He was obliged to fall back again upon giving lessons and concerts. The brilliant success of his spring "academies" encouraged him to arrange four concerts during Advent, immediately after the triumph of Martin's "Cosa rara." At these concerts Mozart introduced a new pianoforte concerto. The many-sidedness of Mozart's activity as a composer during 1786 is astounding.

In November, prompted by his English friends, Kelly, Nancy Storace, and her brother, Stephen Storace, to whom must be added his pupil, Thomas Attwood, Mozart wrote to his father that he had it in view to make a journey to England during the next carnival, provided his father would take charge of his children meanwhile, as Constance would accompany him. (Mozart's third son, Leopold, was born on the 27th of October; he died in the following spring.) The old father energetically refused this proposition, and even made a merit of his refusal in a letter on the subject to

Marianne. It is to be regretted that he was guilty of such heartlessness. The plan therefore had to be given up. Fortunately Mozart was not left long to brood over his disappointment. He received a proposal from his friends in Prague to visit that city, where great triumphs were preparing for his works, and especially "Figaro." Count Johann Joseph Thun sent him an express invitation, and the circumstance of its acceptance by Mozart is the principal cause to which we owe the possession to-day of that masterpiece, "Don Giovanni," which was to reveal to the world in its full splendour the genius of Mozart.

At the beginning of January, 1787, Mozart travelled with Constance to Prague. "Le Nozze di Figaro" had been performed at Prague, and all the talk was about "Figaro." We can understand that wherever the composer appeared he was received with enthusiasm. He played in a musical academy at the theatre to a crowded house. When the programme was finished he continued to play on the pianoforte, and concluded with improvising variations on "Non più andrai." A second concert had the same success. The singer Nancy Storace, told Leopold Mozart that Wolfgang took a thousand florins in Prague. At a representation of "Figaro," excellently rendered by the company of the manager Bondini, Mozart was received by the public with enthusiasm. He himself was particularly pleased with the orchestra on this occasion, which, although it contained no musician of any distinction, yet played with genuine fire and zeal. He wrote a letter to the conductor, Strohbach, thanking the orchestra for its excellent performance. That the composer of "Figaro" should become the hero of the day was what might have been expected. Mozart declared that he would with pleasure write an opera for the people of Prague, who understood him so well and valued him so sincerely. Bondini took him at his word, and concluded an agreement with him, the terms of which were that Mozart bound himself to write an opera for the next season, in consideration of the sum of a hundred ducats. This opera was "Don Giovanni."

On returning to Vienna the composer was once more seized with the desire of visiting England. But the plan again came to nothing. His English friends, the Storaces, brother and sister, and Kelly, travelled thither without him, taking Salzburg on their way, in order to visit the father of their friend. Unfortunately they found Leopold Mozart in a bad state of health. When Wolfgang heard of it he wrote to his father with that sympathy and affection which were a conspicuous feature of his character. He alluded to death, for which he, Wolfgang, was prepared every day, since his dear friend, Count Hatzfeld, died at the age of thirty-one. He did not grieve for him, but rather for himself and for all those who had known him intimately. At the same time he begged his father to write and tell him openly and exactly how he was. It was evidently his intention to travel to Salzburg himself, and see his father once again. However, Leopold Mozart fancied he was getting better, until suddenly, on the 28th of May, death overtook him. A short but wonderfully sympathetic letter, written by Mozart to his sister, tenderly reproaches her with not having told him of the death, although she lived so near her father. At the same time he assures her of his faithful fraternal affection. It was in the midst of impressions such as these that the master began the composition of "Don Giovanni," the libretto of which was written by his friend Da Ponte. But his position in Vienna was made more painful by the fact that he saw his rival Martin preferred before him. Even Dittersdorf stood higher at that time in the favour of the theatrical public than Mozart. The Emperor Joseph, too, openly favoured him. When Dittersdorf left Vienna, in the spring of 1787, the Emperor's interest in German opera vanished. In the autumn the members received notice ; in February of the following year the performances ceased entirely. The list of compositions which Mozart left behind him shows the two splendid string quintets in C major and G minor to have been written in the days which preceded his father's death.

The composition of "Don Giovanni," however, took up the greater part of his time. Towards the end of September he arrived in Prague, probably with the score nearly complete. The manager had found quarters for Mozart and his wife at "The Three Lions," in the Kohlmarkt. On the 3rd of September, a few days before Mozart's departure from Vienna, one of his best friends died—Doctor

Sigmund Barisani, son of the Barisani who was body-physician to the Archbishop of Salzburg, and with whom the Mozart family was on intimate terms. Underneath some verses in praise of Mozart, written by Barisani in his friend's album, Mozart wrote, " This day, the 3rd of September of this same year, I had the misfortune to lose quite unex-pectedly by death this noble man, my dearest, best friend, and the saviour of my life. With him it is well; but with me—with us—with all who knew him intimately—with us, it will never be well until we have the happiness of seeing him again in a better world where we shall never part." In the summer of 1784 Barisani had saved Mozart's life in typhus fever. In the summer of 1787 Mozart was again attacked by fever, and it was only owing to Bari-sani's skill that the journey to Prague did not have to be given up. Barisani did everything in his power to enable Mozart to make the mental and bodily efforts which his compositions required from him. For instance, he induced him always to write standing, and every day to take proper exercise. Mozart, following the doctor's advice, was for some time accustomed to ride early in the morning, but he soon gave up the exercise.

His friends at Prague, particularly the two artists Herr and Madame Duschek, were highly pleased to have Mozart once more with them. Duschek's vineyard at Kossir, in the suburbs of Prague, was Mozart's favourite resort. The stone table is still shown on which he wrote the score of " Don Giovanni," whilst the surrounding company chatted pleasantly and amused themselves with skittles. We have unfortunately no detailed account of Mozart's inter-course with the singers at rehearsal and in respect of their parts. Tradition relates how Mozart taught Teresa Bondini, the manager's sister, who played Zerlina, to utter the famous cry of distress, and also how he had a trifling dispute with the trombone player in the orchestra. The first performance was delayed. In order to show honour to Mozart it was decided to give a representation of " Figaro " in presence of the Archduchess Maria Theresa, who was passing through Prague on her wedding tour as the wife of Prince Anton, of Saxony. One of the ladies of the princess's court tried to thwart this design; but, by imperial command, " Figaro "

I

was given, Mozart conducting on the occasion, and having a new and grand triumph. The first performance of " Don Giovanni " took place on the 29th of October, 1787. On the evening before, the overture was not yet written. Mozart began to sketch it out while drinking a glass of punch, and listening to the amusing tales of his wife. He then took a few hours' rest. Early the next morning, at seven o'clock, the copyist received the overture, with the ink still wet. In the evening the orchestra played it by sight, and so well that Mozart could say to the nearest performer, " To be sure a good many notes have fallen under the desk, but, for all that, the overture has prospered right well." The cast was as follows :—Don Giovanni, Luigi Bassi ; Don Ottavio, Baglioni ; Leporello, Ponziani ; Masetto and Il Commendatore, Guiseppe Lolli. The part of Donna Anna was created by Teresa Saporiti, a spirited singer ; Elvira was played by Caterina Micelli, and Zerlina by Teresa Bondini. The storm of applause which greeted the overture, accompanied the opera to its conclusion. The performance was praised even by Mozart. What the artists lacked in talent was compensated for by the zeal with which, inspired by the master, all worked together. Bondini's partner, Guardasoni, who arranged the scenic effects, was most triumphant, and exclaimed, " Every manager must bless Da Ponte and Mozart ; from henceforth there cannot be any theatrical famine as long as they are alive." Mozart himself must have enjoyed deep heartfelt pleasure on the first and following nights, and stored up many an hour of genuine happiness ; this, indeed, we see from a letter written to Gottfried von Jacquin, in which he wishes that his best friends could only pass one single evening such as his, so that they might share in his pleasure. As Nimetschek tells us, in those days Mozart, when in the circle of his friends, was as simple as a child, and made the most absurd jokes, so as to make them forget with what a celebrated man and great artist they had to do.

It will be asked how it came to pass that Da Ponte selected the story of Don Giovanni as the subject of his libretto. The first suggestion came to him probably from two operas the hero of which had been Don Giovanni, and which had been given at Vienna, Prague, and Venice. In the year 1777 was produced, both at Vienna and Prague, a tragic-comic drama, entitled "Il Convitato di pietra, ossia il Dissoluto," by Vincenzo Righini, and in 1787 at San Mosè, in Venice, "Il Convitato di Pietra," by Gazzaniga. The last-named work had considerable success, and, notwithstanding the fame which in the meantime Mozart's "Don Giovanni" obtained, kept its place on the Italian stage to such a degree that Goethe, who was in Rome at the time, remembered afterwards that "it was performed every night for four weeks, and that no one could be said to have lived who had not witnessed Don Juan roasting in the nether regions, and the commendatore going up to heaven as a blessed spirit." Unfortunately, the text of this opera of Gazzaniga's has not been discovered; we can only conclude, from a fragment of the score preserved by the Musical Society of Vienna, that in all probability Da Ponte made a free use of it in his own libretto. The story of Don Juan originates in Spain, and was first employed by Gabriele Tellez, a contemporary of Lope de Vega, and afterwards by Tirso de Molina. It made its appearance on the Italian stage soon after 1620. An imitation of its treatment by Giliberti at Naples in 1652 was produced in 1657 at the Hôtel de Bourgogne, in Paris. Thenceforward the subject is frequently met with. Molière's comedy-ballet, "Le Festin de Pierre," which appeared on the 16th of February, 1665, is well known. In the eighteenth century the story was again made use of by Goldoni. The English stage also took possession of it. Thomas Shadwell's comedy, "The Libertine Destroyed," had a great success, in spite of the dulness of the treatment. In Germany, Schroeder took up the story of Don Juan, and gave it as an adaptation of Molière's "Festin." It was first employed in opera by Le Tellier in Paris. Lastly, we come to the ballet "Don Juan," composed by Gluck, which was performed at Vienna in 1761. Don Juan therefore is a subject of international dramatic literature to which Mozart's masterpiece has in a manner given its final form.

The chief merit of Da Ponte's libretto lies not in the invention of effective dramatic situations, but in the skilful manner in which he has built up the plot, and made it peculiarly fit for musical treatment. The alternation of arias and *ensembles* in "Don Giovanni" is indubitably artistic, and is a proof that the librettis kept well in view the requirements of the stage.

His text, so wonderfully full of life, presented but one difficulty to a dramatic musician like Mozart. The difficulty lay in the temptation to make single situations too deeply characteristic. He had, in fact, to avoid that which, in most of his other opera libretti, the impulse of self-preservation had in a way compelled him to do. Nowhere has Mozart made such a brilliant display of that fine artistic sense which was a feature of his genius as in the treatment of this libretto. He always knows where to draw the line, and the ease with which his music seems to hit upon the correct expression is marvellous. For that reason he is under no necessity to explain at great length what he wishes to express. The finest example of this is the meeting of Don Giovanni with Zerlina after the chorus in the first finale. The interchange of serious, half-serious, downright comic situations gradually leading up to the tragic end of the hero is, as it were, a mirror held up to the nature of Mozart, who, whilst busy with the most serious things of his art, could jest and make merry in the pleasantest and most careless manner.

Goethe's penetration was not at fault when he observed that Mozart would have been the man to compose his "Faust." "Don Giovanni" is the expression of a universal genius, which could reproduce in music every emotion of the human heart—great and small—with equal truth to nature. For this reason the work never wearies, however familiar it may be. We feel drawn into the very heart, as it were, of each situation as it presents itself; with marvellous consistency the master carries us along with him, always keeping our imagination on the alert. We follow him willingly, for we always feel the ground safe under our feet. Perfection of form is the basis of his highest flight of enthusiasm; but the fetters with which Mozart has bound himself are not perceptible. The master's achievements in "Figaro" in the management of the form of the finale which was so peculiarly his own creation, are child's-play compared to the two finales of "Don Giovanni." He had but to recognize the magnitude of the task before him, to obtain a complete mastery over it. It is interesting to note that Mozart's contemporaries speedily became familiar with the new work of art, and comprehended its greatness. The Vienna public, on hearing "Don Giovanni " for the first time in 1788, was indeed for the moment somewhat startled ; its taste had been spoilt by the humdrum ways of Salieri and other composers. However, approbation grew with every performance, fifteen of which followed each other in the course of the year.

On the 8th of November, during the last days of his stay at Prague, Mozart composed an aria for his friend, Frau Duschek. She locked him up in a summer-house, and declared she would not let him out till the aria was finished. It is observable that this aria, "Bella mia fiamma," although it bears a striking resemblance to the music of "Don Gio-. vanni," yet intrinsically differs from it. It was simply calculated for the concert-room. Mozart, moreover, revenged himself in it for his friend's act of violence, by introducing into the andante a succession of intervals which put to a severe test the singer's purity of intonation. History does not relate whether Frau Duschek stood the test.

On Mozart's return to Vienna an opportunity arose for the Emperor Joseph to bestow a mark of distinction upon him. Gluck died on the 15th of November, and on the 7th of December Mozart was appointed " Chamber Musician," with a salary of eight hundred florins, and the title of "Capell-meister in the actual service of his I. R. Majesty." That the salary was not higher—Gluck had had two thousand florins—is ascribed to the influence of the valet Strack, by whom the Emperor was continually advised. In the sequel Mozart proved much less discontented with the pay than with the insufficiency of work required of him. In an official statement of his salary he wrote against the amount, " Too much for what I do, too little for what I could do." However, the hint remained unnoticed in both respects.

In January, 1788, Mozart had to compose dances for the ball in the " Redoutensaal." As yet there was no question of performing "Don Giovanni" in Vienna. War with Turkey threatened to break out. Patriotic demonstrations were the order of the day. Mozart was not behindhand. He composed Gleim's war song : " Ich möchte wohl der Kaiser sein," which was sung by Baumann, the comedian, on the 7th of March, in the Leopoldstadt theatre, and was received with great enthusiasm by the audience. By the 28th of February the Emperor had already left Vienna for the headquarters of the army, but had previously given the necessary orders for the performance of "Don Giovanni." At last, on the 7th of May, 1788, the representation took place, with Albertarelli as Don Giovanni, Benucci as Leporello, and Morella as Ottavio ; Donna Anna was played by Mozart's sister-in-law, Aloysia Lange, Elvira by Caterina Cavalieri, and Zerlina by Luisa Mombelli. As has been said already, the success of the opera increased with every performance. Da Ponte relates that the Emperor said of it, "This is no food for the teeth of my Viennese !" and that Mozart when he heard of it exclaimed, "We must let them have time to digest it !" The anecdote is *ben trovato ma non vero*, for the Emperor did not return to Vienna till December, when the success of the opera was brilliantly decided. The additions made by Mozart in "Don Giovanni" before its first representation on the Vienna stage consisted of an aria for Masetto, a short aria for Ottavio ("Dalla sua pace"), a duet for Zerlina and Leporello, and the recitative and aria for Elvira, so much admired at the present day—"In quali eccessi o Numi."

Notwithstanding the appointment at court, and the success of "Don Giovanni," Mozart's pecuniary circumstances were not improved. Had not one of his masonic brethren, Puchberg, now and again helped him out, he would have had to struggle with the direst necessity. It was during this time of distress that his great symphonies in C major and G minor were written, of which Richard Wagner enthusiastically speaks in the following terms :—"He breathed into his instruments the passionate longing of the human voice to which his genius with all-pervading love inclined him. The inexhaustible stream of rich harmony he led into the heart of the melody, as if in restless anxiety to impart to it, by way of compensation for its exposition by instruments only, the depth of feeling and fervour of the human voice. Thus he raised the capacity of instrumental music for vocal expression to a height which enabled it to embrace the whole depths of the infinite yearning of the heart." Mozart received an incitement to fresh diligence through that zealous friend of music, Baron van Swieten, who had made him acquainted with the works of Bach and Handel in 1782. At the private performances, which Van Swieten instituted in the great hall of the court library, before an audience composed of invited guests, Mozart had acted as conductor since 1787. In this capacity he was commissioned to prepare an arrangement of Handel's "Acis and Galatea," which was produced in November, 1788, and made a great impression upon the audience. It was followed in March of the next year by the "Messiah," and later by "Alexander's Feast" and the "Ode for St. Cecilia's Day." In these arrangements Mozart had it in view to make an effective substitution of wind instruments for the organ. The notion that he wanted to improve Handel must be entirely set aside. His object was simply to make the representation of the works referred to possible at Van Swieten's entertainments. That these arrangements afterwards supplanted Handel's originals must not be laid to Mozart's charge, although it is evident that the popularity of the great oratorio-composer in Germany dated from their publication.

Mozart's employment on these masterpieces was of great importance to his further development. It gave him abundance of work, but he received no pay from Van Swieten. He was therefore obliged to contemplate a new tour. Another inducement to this was the circumstance that Prince Lichnowsky, husband of the Countess Thun, offered to take him to Berlin in his carriage. At Berlin the prince could be of great use to Mozart with King Frederick William II., who was well known for his love of music and his liberality. On the 8th of April, 1789, Mozart set out with the prince. At Prague he heard from his old friend Ramm that the King of Prussia was anxiously inquiring for him, and already expected him. The travellers entered Dresden on the 12th of April. On the 14th Mozart played before the court, and received a present of a hundred ducats. He also played in private circles, and came off victor from a trial of skill with the distinguished pianoforte and organ player, T. W. Hässler, of Erfurt. While at Berlin he made the acquaintance of Judge Koerner, father of the poet, whose sister-in-law, Dora Stock, drew Mozart's portrait in crayon. At Leipsic he became acquainted with Doles, Cantor of St. Thomas's School, and, through him, with the young author Rochlitz, to whom we owe the record of a number of interesting traits of Mozart's life, which he afterwards published in the Leipsic *Allgemeine Musikalische Zeitung.* Musical life in Leipsic was even at that time a stirring one. Much chamber-music was played, and Mozart was naturally admitted as a welcome guest into the best houses of the town. The violinist Berger used to say in his old days, when occasion offered, " In this I had the honour to accompany the great Mozart." On the 24th of April Mozart played the organ in the Church of St. Thomas. The church was crowded. In his honour, Doles caused the St. Thomas's scholars to sing the cantata, " Sing unto the Lord a new song." Surprised at this polyphony of vocal writing, previously unknown to him, Mozart exclaimed, " Really, here is something from which one can learn much!" He studied diligently some motets by Bach from the voice parts, as no score was at hand. The evening before his departure he was at Doles' house, and in very good spirits. His hosts, who were sad with the prospect of approaching separation, asked him for a few lines of remembrance. At first Mozart would not agree to the request, but he afterwards asked for a piece of music-paper, tore it in two, and then wrote for about five or six minutes. One half he gave to the father, Doles, the other half to the son. On one piece was a fine canon for three parts, without words, very melancholy, and written in long notes. On the other there was also a canon for three voices, without words, but in quavers, and very lively. It being remarked that both could be sung at the same time, Mozart wrote under one canon the words, " Farewell, we shall meet again," and under the other, " Don't cry like old women." Unfortunately the double canon has been lost.

Mozart now continued his journey to Berlin, and thence went straight to the king at Potsdam. Frederick William II. possessed able musicians at his court, among them Reichardt and Duport, and he himself played well upon the violoncello. He received Mozart very kindly, the " Entführung" having made him acquainted with his genius. The little intrigues which Duport contrived against him came to nothing. After some days had elapsed, the king questioned Mozart as to his opinion of the Berlin Capelle. Mozart frankly replied, " The capelle contains great virtuosi ; still if the gentlemen were together (that is played together), they might do better." While at Berlin, Mozart was persuaded to pay a second visit to Leipsic, where he wanted to give a concert. He reached Leipsic on the 8th of May. At the rehearsal of one of his symphonies, he had a slight dispute with the musicians, but when the work was performed at the concert it went well. Unfortunately the pecuniary results of the concert did not realize his expectations. The evening of his return to Berlin the "Entführung" was performed. During the representation, which took place on the 19th of May, Mozart drew the attention of the audience upon himself by calling out aloud to the second violin, who was playing a wrong note, "D——n you, will you take D?" On this same evening he accidentally became acquainted with young Ludwig Tieck, who was enthusiastic in his praise of Mozart's operas.

It happened that Hummel, who had been Mozart's pupil since 1787, gave a concert in Berlin without being aware of his master's presence in that city. When he perceived him amongst the audience, he rushed up to him, and embraced him in the most cordial manner, as Hummel's widow related afterwards to Otto Jahn. On the 26th of May Mozart played before the queen. He did not give a concert of his own at Berlin. The king sent him a hundred ducats (Friedrichsdor), with a request that he would write him some quartets. The profits arising from the tour were not large, as we have seen, and moreover Mozart, with his usual good-nature, had lent a hundred florins to a stranger he met on his way. He wrote to his wife that upon his return she must rejoice more over him than over the money he brought. Mozart left Berlin on the 28th of May, travelling to Vienna by way of Dresden and Prague. Before his departure the king offered him the post of capellmeister at Berlin, with a salary of three thousand thalers. Mozart refused the offer, saying, "Shall I forsake my good emperor?" On his return home he informed the Emperor of the proposal, but it led to no improvement in his position at Vienna. Fortunately, King Frederick William sent him a present of a hundred ducats and a gold snuff-box for the D major quartet, which was finished in June.

In the meantime Mozart's wife became seriously ill, and this entailed upon him fresh care and expense. The only thing that the Emperor Joseph did for him was to commission him to write a new opera, for which Da Ponte was to supply the text. The piece was called "Cosi fan tutte, ossia la scuola degli amanti." In December Mozart was busy with its composition, and in January, 1790, it was completed. The libretto, which was substantially invented by Da Ponte, although it had some foundation in an anecdote of that time, seems to have been considered a feeble one; but in spite of this, Mozart's music was greatly applauded. Although it does not rank as high as that of "Don Giovanni," still many portions of it bear witness to the master's progress. The performances of the new opera were interrupted by the illness and death, on the 20th of February, of the Emperor Joseph. Upon the accession to the throne of Leopold II., Mozart made an attempt to be appointed second Capellmeister with Salieri ; but again to no purpose. He then applied to the town council of Vienna to be associated with Capellmeister Hofmann at St. Stephen's. The request was granted, and the Capellmeistership secured to him in case Hofmann died. Hofmann, however, outlived Mozart. Thus the great master's circumstances daily became worse. His wife continued in delicate health for a long time. Expenses increased, and the earnings became less. The number of his pupils too diminished. In May he had only two pupils, and was obliged to ask his friends to help him to more. Under such circumstances even his friend Puchberg, ready as he always was for self-sacrifice, could not extricate him from his difficulties, and Mozart was compelled to have recourse to moneylenders. As might be supposed, his powers of composition suffered, and this was what troubled him most. Two string quartets and the arrangements of the "Ode for St. Cecilia's Day," and "Alexander's Feast," are the sole products of the year 1790.

The coronation of Leopold II., which was to take place on the 9th of October, at Frankfort, induced Mozart to make a new tour having Frankfort for its destination. As he could not join the imperial musicians, who, fifteen in number, with Salieri and Umlauf at their head, were ordered to attend the festivities at Frankfort, Mozart travelled in a private carriage with his brother-in-law, the violinist Hofer. To obtain the necessary funds for the journey, he was obliged to pawn his plate. Mozart and Hofer left Vienna on the 23rd of September, and after a journey of six days reached Frankfort, where, on the 14th of October, Mozart gave a special concert in the Stadttheater, as it appears with no particular success. He afterwards made an excursion to Mayence, where Tischbein painted a half-length portrait, much praised for its like-ness by contemporaries. On his return journey, Mozart passed through Mannheim. Here, on the 24th of October, he had the gratification of witnessing an excellent performance of his "Figaro." At Munich, where he stayed with his old friend Albert, he fell in with many old friends who welcomed him affectionately. The Elector desired him to play at a concert given in honour of the King of Naples. "A fine thing for the Court of Vienna," Mozart writes to his wife, "that the king should have to hear me in foreign lands." At Vienna the master had not once been sent for to play before the king, a cause of great annoyance to him. When Mozart returned to Vienna, he found his old friend, Joseph Haydn, on the eve of starting for London, he having been engaged by Salomon for concerts there. Salomon also entered into preliminary negotiations with Mozart, which unfortunately never came to anything. Mozart was doubtful concerning the advisability of Haydn's journey to London. "Papa," said he, "you are not fitted for the great world, and you speak too few languages." To which Haydn re-plied, "But my language is understood all over the world." At their parting on the 15th of December, both men were moved to tears. "I fear, my father, we are saying our last good-bye!" Mozart exclaimed. His words were prophetic. They never saw each other again.

With care and anxiety for the continual ill-health of his wife, who besides was expecting another confinement, the new year 1791 began for Mozart. It is wonderful to think that in this—the last year of his life—he should have accom-plished so much work. Among the compositions belonging to this period is the beautiful "Ave verum." On the 4th of March he performed once more publicly, at a concert given by the clarinet-player Bähr. He had not played in public in Vienna since 1788, and this was his last appearance. About this time the manager, Schikaneder, an old acquaintance of his Salzburg days, now reduced by unfortunate speculations,

applied to him.  He gave him a subject for an opera, of
which he entertained great hopes.  Mozart's inclination to
opera came back to him, and he agreed to the proposal the
more readily as it was urged by a brother mason.  Schikaneder imparted to Mozart the scheme of " Zauberflöte," and,
in order to keep his eye upon the composer, gave him the use
of the garden pavilion in the centre court of the Stahrem-
berg House, auf der Wieden, close to his theatre.  Here,
and in Josephsdorf, on the Kahlenberg, Mozart composed "Die
Zauberflöte," to which he gave the name "a German opera."
The little summer-house now stands in the garden of the
Capuzinerberg, at Salzburg.  Da Ponte made a proposal to
Mozart at this time to go with him to London, and seek their
fortune with Italian opera.  Mozart replied that he must
have six weeks first to finish " Die Zauberflöte," but to this
Da Ponte would not agree.

In the middle of July, when Mozart had advanced so far with
"Die Zauberflöte" that the rehearsals could begin, he received
a visit from a man, to him unknown, tall, haggard-looking,
and clad in grey.  The stranger handed him an anonymous
letter, which contained an inquiry as to the sum for which
he would compose a Requiem, and the length of time he would
require for it.  By his wife's advice, Mozart consented to do
the work, and received from the same messenger fifty ducats,
according to others a hundred, with the promise of an addi-
tional sum upon completion.  He was to make no attempt to
discover who it was that had given him the order.  It afterwards transpired that the mysterious patron was Count Franz
von Walsegg, of Stuppach, and the requiem was intended for
his wife, Anna von Flammberg, who died on the 14th of
February, 1791.  The messenger was his steward, Leutgeb.
The count delighted in these anonymous commissions.  He
would often perform compositions obtained in such a manner,
with his officers and servants, and would afterwards make
those present guess the composer.  Generally the count
himself was named.  The score which he received from
Mozart he copied out again, and wrote upon the copy, "Com-
posta dal Conte Walsegg."  The Requiem was performed on
the 14th of December, 1793, under the count's direction.

In the meantime, the Bohemian nobles invited to the
coronation of Leopold II. as King of Bohemia commissioned

Mozart to compose Metastasio's festival opera, "La Clemenza di Tito." A few weeks only were allowed him for
the work.

On the 26th of July, 1791, Constance gave birth to a son,
baptized Wolfgang Amadeus. Towards the end of August,
when Mozart and his wife were about to set out for Prague,
the mysterious messenger again made his appearance, and
obtained a promise that the Requiem should be the first
work undertaken by the master on his return from Prague.
Mozart had called in to his assistance in the composition of
"La Clemenza" Franz Süssmayer, a young composer, who
was to write the "recitativo secco." The original score has
no "recitativo secco," and is, moreover, entirely in Mozart's
handwriting, so that it is very probable that Süssmayer added
the recitatives.

On the 6th of September the opera was brought
out with great splendour. It did not, however, please the
empress, and was altogether somewhat coldly received by
the public, generally so enthusiastic for Mozart. Full of
disappointment, ill in body, and in the most melancholy
frame of mind, Mozart returned home. "Titus" is an "opera
seria." The libretto, written by Metastasio in 1734 for
Caldara, was again and again set to music by a formidable
succession of composers. Catterino Mazzola, the court poet
of Saxony, made a few alterations in the text for Mozart.
Substantially the libretto, which, even in Mozart's time was
antiquated, preserved its original character. Although
Mozart's dramatic talent cannot be said to fail in any
number of the score, yet the piece presents but little which
will bear comparison with his other important works. He
was pressed to complete the opera in the shortest possible
space of time, and the result is that both design and execution bear many a trace of hurry. But there is one number
which reaches the standard we have a right to expect from
the composer of "Don Giovanni." This is the first finale,
the grand features of which unroll before us an historical
picture. All the characters in the opera appear in this finale
in which they give vent to their horror at the murder of the
Emperor Titus, committed, as is supposed, by conspirators
during the burning of the Capitol. The chorus mingles in
the lamentations over the dead emperor, and the whole

produces an effect which, from a musical and from a dramatic point of view, is deeply moving. The opinion of contemporaries concerning the work was much divided. Some, like Niemetschek, regarded it in its æsthetic aspects as Mozart's most finished work. Others considered the whole dull and barren. A very able verdict is that pronounced by Rochlitz. He says, "Not being a god, Mozart found himself compelled either to produce a work which should be mediocre throughout, or else one of which the principal theme alone should be very good, the less interesting parts slightly worked in, and the great mass merely written to suit the taste of the day. He chose the latter."

When Mozart, depressed and in ill-health, had returned to Vienna, he sent his wife to Baden for her recovery. He himself was occupied with the completion of "Die Zauberflöte," and with the "Requiem." The overture and the introduction to the second act of the new opera were finished on the 28th of September, and on the 30th the first performance took place. The work did not have the success hoped for, although, at its conclusion, Mozart was called before the curtain. Schikaneder nevertheless gave repetitions of the opera in quick succession, and it became more and more firmly established in the favour of the public. "Die Zauberflöte" "drew" as none of Mozart's earlier operas had done. In October it was performed twenty-four times; the hundredth performance took place on the 23rd of November, 1792; and the two-hundredth on the 22nd of November, 1795.

The subject of "Die Zauberflöte" was originally borrowed from the story of "Lulu, or the Magic Flute," in Wieland's 'Dschinnistan.'' Schikaneder had half of the first act ready, when he heard that a piece was in preparation at the Leopoldstadt theatre, bearing the title, "Caspar der Fagottist, oder die Zauberzither," which was founded upon the same story. This piece was performed on the 8th of June with great success. In order not quite to give up the scheme of "Die Zauberflöte," suitable alterations had to be made in the construction of the piece. Thus instead of a wicked sorcerer, as in the play referred to, we have a noble-minded philosopher, Sarastro, who brings Tamino to his side, leads him in the paths of wisdom and virtue, and rewards him with the hand of Pamina. At the same time a popular element was introduced in the apotheosis of the order of Freemasonry, which under Leopold II. had fallen into discredit, and was looked upon with suspicion, an apotheosis on the stage by means of which the good and noble qualities of Freemasonry were demonstrated to the public in a generally intelligible manner. Perhaps a direct influence had been brought to bear upon Schikaneder by the order. The design is said to have been due to a Brunswick littérateur of the name of Gieseke, whom Schikaneder employed as an actor and chorus-singer. Gieseke had before this written the libretto of Wranitsky's "Oberon," which had brought him a certain reputation. Schikaneder apparently made use of Gieseke's work as a foundation. The characters of Papageno and Papagena are his own invention. Tasteless and absurd as many things in the libretto now seem to us, the immense success of the play justifies the opinion of Goethe, who, while acknowledging that "Die Zauberflöte" is full of improbabilities and jokes which might not be to every one's taste, says, "It must at any rate be conceded to the author that he understood in the highest degree the art of working by contrast, and that he produced by this means great theatrical effects." But it is certainly to Mozart's music that the work owes its chief success. The analogy between Freemasonry and the mysteries of Isis must have exercised a great charm over him. As a mason he has thrown wonderful earnestness into this portion of the opera. The dignified and sublime elements here placed in juxtaposition with vulgarity, Mozart has treated with predilection, giving them characteristic musical expression. In this respect the German text was of great importance. Widely distinct from the laboured poetry of former libretti, it offered no hindrance to the composer in his choice of those musical forms which might best express the situation. The perfect mastery he had obtained over his art culminated at the close of his active life in a triumph rarely permitted to mortals. He opened the door to a national art, and has thereby earned the gratitude, not only of Germans, but of all nations.

When "Die Zauberflöte" was finished, Mozart concentrated his whole strength upon the "Requiem." The effort increased the indisposition which had never left him since his visit to Prague. No wonder that melancholy, to which till now he had been an entire stranger, took complete possession of him.

His wife did all she could to distract his thoughts. One day as they were sitting in the Prater, Mozart began to weep, and declared he was writing the "Requiem" for himself. "I feel," he said, "I am not going to last much longer. Some one has certainly given me poison. I cannot get rid of this idea." His wife, alarmed by his words, took away from him the score of the "Requiem."

Under the skilful treatment of Dr. Closset, Mozart recovered sufficiently to compose for a Masonic festival the little cantata, "Laut verkünde unsre Freude." It was finished on the 15th of November, and is the last work of the master entered by his own hand in the list of his compositions. He himself conducted the cantata when sung in lodge. The applause it won pleased him, and raised his spirits, and he even acknowledged the groundlessness of his suspicion of poison. He again set to work zealously upon the "Requiem." But his former despondency soon came back. His hands and feet began to swell, and he had occasional fits of vomiting. The porter of the alehouse, "The Silver Serpent," in the Kaerntnerstrasse, Joseph Deiner by name, related how ill Mozart looked when he came to order some wood. Next morning when Deiner came, he found Mozart in bed. With scarcely audible voice Mozart said to the faithful servant, "Joseph, to-day we can do nothing—to-day we have to do with doctors and apothecaries." On the 28th of November his condition was so critical that Dr. Closset had a consultation with the head physician of the great hospital, Dr. Sallaba. Mozart's only consolation during his sufferings was to hear of the repeated performances of "Die Zauberflöte." He would follow the representations in spirit, laying his watch beside him, and saying, "Now the first act is over. Now they are come to the place, 'The great Queen of Night,'" &c. Only the day before his death he expressed a wish that he might hear "Die Zauberflöte" once more. He hummed to himself the song, "Der Vogelfänger bin ich ja" Capellmeister Roser, who happened to be with him, went to the harpsichord and played and sang the song, which appeared greatly to cheer Mozart. Nevertheless the "Requiem" occupied him continually. As soon as he had finished a piece, he had it rehearsed by the friends who happened to be present. At two o'clock in the afternoon of the day before his death, Schack, who was the first Tamino, sang soprano, Mozart himself contralto, Hofer, his brother-in-law, tenor, and Gerl, who was the first Sarastro, bass. At the "Lacrymosa" Mozart began to weep violently, and laid down the score. Towards evening, when his sister-in-law, Sophie Haibl, came in, Mozart begged her to remain and help Constance, as he felt death approaching. She went out again just to tell her mother and to fetch a priest. When she returned she found Mozart in lively conversation with Süssmayer. "Did I not say that I was writing the 'Requiem' for myself?" he said; and then, with a sure presentiment of approaching death, he charged his wife instantly to inform Albrechtsberger, on whom his post at St. Stephen's would devolve. Late in the evening he lost consciousness. But the "Requiem" still seemed to occupy him, and he puffed out his cheeks as if he would imitate a wind instrument, the "Tuba mirum spargens sonum." Towards midnight his eyes became fixed. Then he appeared to fall into slumber, and about one o'clock in the morning of the 5th of December he died.

The two servants prepared his body for burial. People came in crowds to lament over him. His sudden death taught the Viennese in a moment what they had lost. One of the next numbers of the *Wiener Zeitung* contained a few lines recording the death as one through which the noble art of music had sustained a loss to be estimated by the distinguished works he had written. Salieri is understood to have said, when he heard of his rival's death, "It is indeed a pity for the great genius, but well for us that he is dead; for had he lived longer, no one would have given us a crust of bread for our compositions." Schikaneder was most deeply affected, and declared, "His spirit follows me everywhere; he stands constantly before my eyes."

Constance broke down beneath the pressure of the sad event. In her despair she lay in her husband's bed, that she might die of the same illness, the peculiar character of which indicated malignant typhus fever, a disease from which Mozart had previously suffered. Baron van Swieten hastened, as soon as the news reached him, to Constance's assistance. He took upon himself the arrangements for the funeral, which he conducted in the most economical manner possible. It never entered his head that the least he, a rich man, could do for the great artist who, moreover, had contributed to his renown, was to provide him with a decent funeral. On the 6th of December the corpse was brought from the house of mourning, in the Rauhensteingasse, to St. Stephen's, and was there in the Kreuzcapelle consecrated. Owing to the bad weather, only a few friends were present. It is some satisfaction to know that besides Van Swieten, Roser, and the violoncellist Orsler, Salieri was among the mourners. With umbrellas up, the friends surrounded the simple bier as it was about to be borne through the Schulerstrasse to the graveyard of St. Mark. The weather becoming worse every moment, the mourners returned to the Stubenthor, and no friend, only the attendants of the cemetery, stood by the grave of the man who by his art had prepared such joy and pleasure for his fellow-creatures. He was buried in a so-called "common grave."

When Mozart's widow, a few weeks afterwards, having recovered from her prostration, visited the cemetery, she found there a new grave-digger, who was unable to point out her husband's grave. All search proved fruitless. A singular report was current that the corpse had been violated in order to obtain the skull for some physiognomist. But nothing certain is known, for the place of burial even cannot be pointed to with any certainty. Mozart's widow remained with her children in comfortless circumstances. She obtained a private audience of the Emperor Leopold, and laid her sad case before him. In this way she personally refuted the malicious reports which were circulated concerning her husband immediately after his death. It was said that he had contracted debts to the amount of thirty thousand florins by his extravagance. The Emperor was convinced of the groundlessness of this illnatured tale, when Mozart's widow assured him that with three thousand florins she could satisfy all claims, and that even these debts had been incurred through illness, confinements, and such like causes. Leopold II. advised her to arrange a concert, to which he contributed so generously that all the debts could be paid. The "Requiem," Mozart's dying composition, he left incomplete. His widow entrusted to Süssmayer the task of finishing such portions as were imperfect. In this way the score was made complete, and handed over to Count Walsegg. The similarity of Mozart's and Süssmayer's handwritings was so great that the whole might be taken for the work of one man. When afterwards copies were circulated, and made known through statements in the public press, Count Walsegg brought an action against Mozart's widow, but was satisfied with copies of some unpublished works of Mozart. A great deal has been written as to the genuineness of the " Requiem." But it is now finally acknowledged by all the world that the greatest part of it is the work of Mozart.

The neglect of his contemporaries in taking care of his grave was atoned for by a grateful posterity. On the 5th of December, 1859, a monument to Mozart, erected by the city of Vienna in the churchyard of St. Mark, was unveiled. It was executed by the sculptor, Hans Gasser, and represents the Muse mourning, in her right hand the score of the " Requiem," and in her left a wreath of laurel. Mozart's works are piled upon the ground. On the pedestal is Mozart's portrait, with a short inscription. Seventeen years before, Schwanthaler's bronze statue of Mozart was unveiled in the square of St. Michael, at Salzburg. It is one of the finest pieces of sculpture produced by modern German art. The expression of the face, which is looking upwards, is calm and noble, the head is turned a little to one side. In his hand he holds a sheet of music, upon which are the words " Tuba mirum," from the " Requiem."

\*        \*        \*        \*        \*        \*

In 1862 there appeared in Leipsic, published by Breitkopf and Härtel, the " Chronologisch-thematisches Verzeichniss sämmtlicher Tonwerke Wolfg. Amad. Mozart's," by Dr. Ludwig Ritter von Koechel. Reference has been made to it in these pages by means of numbers in conjunction with the name Koechel. Besides the classified catalogue of Mozart's works, we owe to this enthusiastic admirer of the great master another monument, which renders to Mozart the highest homage. At his instigation, and aided by his princely liberality, the firm of Breitkopf and Härtel undertook in 1876 the " Erste Kritische Gesammtausgabe der Werke Mozart's," which has quite recently been brought to a successful end.

www.ingramcontent.com/pod-product-compliance
Lightning Source LLC
Chambersburg PA
CBHW030606270326
41927CB00007B/1065